the successful manager's gameplan

100 DAYS TO BECOME A WINNER

Richard Koch

An imprint of Pearson Education

London · New York · San Francisco · Toronto · Sydney
Tokyo · Singapore · Hong Kong · Cape Town · Madrid
Paris · Milan · Munich · Amsterdam

PEARSON EDUCATION LIMITED

Head Office:
Edinburgh Gate
Harlow
Essex CM20 2JE
Tel: +44 (0)1279 623623
Fax: +44 (0)1279 431059

London Office:
128 Long Acre
London WC2E 9AN
Tel: +44 (0)20 7447 2000
Fax: +44 (0)20 7836 4286

Website www.business-minds.com

First published in Great Britain in 1994

This edition published 2000

British Library Cataloguing in Publication Data
A Cip catalogue record for this book can be obtained from the British Library.

ISBN 0 273 63545 X

10 9 8 7 6 5 4

Typeset by Northern Phototypesetting Co. Ltd, Bolton
Printed and bound in Great Britain by Bell and Bain Ltd, Glasgow

The Publishers' policy is to use paper manufactured from sustainable forests.

This book is dedicated to my parents,
Don and Phil

Contents

■

Preface

■

This book is for people stepping up into a new job as a boss: where you have responsibility for leading others. It could be your first time as a boss, or your twentieth. The job could be anything: switchboard supervisor in a small firm, head chef, police sergeant, chief fund raiser in a charity, factory foreman, shop manager, managing director of a publisher's, head of the French subsidiary of a multinational giant, cabinet minister, TV producer or the chairman of BP. Each year millions of people face the same challenge of starting a job as a new boss.

Despite the forest of management books available, none tells you what to do as a new boss. You might think this is because the variety of jobs and organisations means there are no general principles for a new boss; but you would be wrong. The similarities outweigh the differences. All new bosses have to make their mark. All have to satisfy outside forces – customers and/or their bosses – which they cannot control. All have money at their disposal, but never enough. All also have people whom they can use, but never (outside a concentration camp) totally control. They are all in uncharted water, uncertain how to proceed, vulnerable to winds and waves they have never experienced before.

So they need a guide book to help them, and here it is.

Being a new boss is difficult. You can be sure that at least one of your people (whom I will call 'direct reports', 'staff', or 'team members', rather than the old-fashioned 'subordinates') thinks that they should have got the job instead of you. They may even be right about this. Even if they are not, they may know the lie of the land in your empire a great deal better than you: its quagmires, quicksands and sloughs of despond. They will be watching you for signs of ignorance or weakness, for evidence that you are not up to the job.

Your bosses will initially be more favourably disposed to you: they will be looking for evidence that they made the right decision in appointing you. But these days few excuses are made for the new leader who is less than foot perfect from the outset.

You will have to learn how your team operates best. You will have to satisfy difficult customers and to cope with marauding competitors. Worst of all, you will have to wrestle with the most volatile and capricious beast of all – yourself, and your expectations, hopes, fears and self-doubts.

And you will have to do all this, not in a leisurely laboratory or an inviolate ivory tower, but in the hard heat of battle and crisis. From day one there will be confrontations and entreaties from your staff. Just when you are quietly trying to accomplish something important, they will arrive to interrupt, badger and plead.

'Let me get one thing straight from the start,' they will demand. Or, 'I need to explain my personal situation.' Or (more subtly), 'Here's how I can help you, but watch out for X.' And whatever they say to your face, you can be sure that there is much more, and worse, being whispered by the coffee machine, bandied around in the pub and exchanged over the phone.

Your predecessor's sins of omission and commission – the hidden timebombs, the hostages to fortune, the implicit alliances, the covert compromises, the ill will with other parts of the organisation, the failures to invest for the future, slack standards and deferred difficult decisions – will pop up to bite you when you least expect them. You will be trying to grapple with something you can only half see and a quarter understand. And yet you will be expected to be the fount of all wisdom and the source of all decisions.

In the face of all this, what on earth are you expected to do? Should you be assertive or easy going? Do you concentrate on actions, even if this means that you may get it wrong? Should you try to change everything from day one or let sleeping dogs lie? Do you keep your own counsel or communicate like crazy? Should you analyse the problems and opportunities from first principles, wait until you have all the information you need or follow your instinct on what's important, even though it's only your opinion? Do you side with the dominant faction in your staff or remain detached? Should you try to develop consensus or do what you think is right?

There are no right or wrong answers to these questions. It all depends: on you, your team, your customers, your competitors, your bosses and the culture of your firm. This variety and ambiguity may explain why no one has been foolhardy enough to write a book like this before. But take heart. There are some lessons which can be learnt by observing the differences between successful and unsuccessful new bosses. There are some general principles which, with a little intelligence and sensitivity on your part, will tell you what to look out for and guide you towards the right answer in each circumstance.

So it is possible to construct a manual to help the new boss – a sort of illustrated guide book to the country you have just entered. It is important to understand the limitations and uses of such a guide book. It will not give you simple rules to follow, regardless of the terrain. Rather it will help you diagnose what is going on, it will provoke thought about which direction you want to take, it will help you work out the odds on success for any given route and it will challenge you to exert leadership.

This guide book, then, will not tell you whether or when to head for the opera, the art gallery, the park, the restaurant or the racetrack. But it will help you to work this out for yourself and will tell you how to get to each of these once you have decided your preference. It will point out the cost of each option and the pitfalls on the way, and point out the most cost-effective and enjoyable way of getting there.

This guide book's style is relaxed and often light hearted, but do not be deceived. I take your responsibilities as seriously as you do. I am concerned to advance your interests, certainly, but also those of your unit or company, and of the broader society in which it operates. The book is sceptical and grounded in experience, but it is not cynical. Work should be fun for you and your team. And in some way, large or small, it should advance the cause of humanity: provide basic goods or services, raise standards of quality and delivery, create extra value, satisfy primary needs or provide colour and variety. You can help to do this by being a better prepared, and better, boss.

1

Before you begin: home

Your new job and your partner

A new job is a good time to think again about the relationship between your home life and your work life. Any job as a new boss is demanding. The support, or otherwise, that you receive at home can be as crucial to your success in the new job as anything that happens at work. This chapter will help you diagnose whether your home base is likely to be supportive or to create difficulties, and supplies some thoughts on how to secure the domestic front before you venture out into the new job.

Some readers will live alone and not have one primary relationship, and if you are in this category you can skip lightly through this chapter or ignore it altogether. For everyone else the relationship you have with your partner should be considered explicitly and carefully. After you have read this chapter, you should ask your partner to review it as well, so that he or she is aware of the type of relationship you have and the impact of your new job, as a basis for discussion between you.

Portfolio partnership

I have adapted this phrase from Charles Handy, who discusses the 'portfolio marriage' in his stimulating book,

The Age of Unreason, Arrow Books, especially pages 155–67. The ideas behind 'portfolio marriage' are applicable to all primary relationships between two people, whatever their marital status. The basic point is that relationships should be adapted to the work requirements of either or both of the partners. Failure to think through the implications can damage both the relationship and performance at work.

Each of us has certain personality traits that mean we are most comfortable with ways of interacting with our partner and his or her career position in a certain way. Sometimes this fits with the job situation and sometimes it doesn't. If it doesn't, there are ways of adapting job requirements, the domestic circumstances and each partner's behaviour to get a better fit. In many cases, without a better fit, you will fail at work or your relationship will come under strain, and perhaps end. For someone starting a new job the dangers should be taken seriously. The good news is that if you are aware of the patterns you can take certain actions to mitigate or remove the difficulties that would otherwise arise. The idea behind 'portfolio partnership' is that you should have a variety (a portfolio) of patterns of behaviour which you deploy at different times in your career and that of your partner. That way you are more likely to make a success of both your job and your relationship.

CHARLES HANDY'S FOUR PERSONALITY AND BEHAVIOUR TYPES

Handy's research identified four types of personality or behaviour based on two dimensions:

- Achievement and Dominance (the need to succeed, and have power and influence), which could either be high or low; and

- succourance and nurturance (the desire to help and support, and take care of someone) versus autonomy (the desire to do your own thing).

He then created a matrix to typify four different types:

Need for achievement and dominance		Need to help, support and take care of others	Need for autonomy
	High	A INVOLVED	B THRUSTERS
	Low	D CARERS	C LONERS

Source: Adapted from Charles Handy, *The Age of Unreason*

WHAT PATTERN ARE YOU IN?

Type A, the Involved, are both achieving and dominant, but also interested in helping and caring for people. Type B, the Thrusters, are archetypal yuppies, ambitious, hard working, but with little time or inclination to help others and a strong drive towards autonomy. Type C, the Loners, score low on everything except autonomy: unambitious, but not social or caring either. Type D, the Carers, are not interested in personal achievement or dominance but want to help others.

You probably do not need a personality test to place either

yourself or your partner on this matrix, in terms of your/his/her personality and preferred behaviour trait today. Go ahead now and classify yourself and your partner.

Without worrying about who comes first in the sequence (you or your partner), there are ten possible combinations for you and your partner. These are AA, AB, AC, AD, BB, BC, BD, CC, CD, DD. Let us consider some of these patterns and the potential difficulties in relation to your new job.

The most common pattern: BD

Let us assume that you are a B (Thruster) and your partner is a D (Carer). This is ideal from your point of view, since your partner can take care of the home base and provide support to you during a time when professional demands on you are at a peak. If your partner does not have a demanding, full-time job, the BD mix is ideal from his or her viewpoint also. The old-fashioned stereotype of the happily married couple is one example of the BD combination: the man is the bread-winner, while the woman runs the home and cares for the children. Nowadays this combination could be the other way round. If it suits both partners, it clearly works. (If you are a B and your partner a D, you may feel tempted to say that there is no problem and skip to the end of this chapter. This would be fine if your partner forever stayed satisfied with the D role and you always have a demanding job at which you are successful. You might pause, however, to consider the need for another pattern if and when either of these changed.)

The AA pattern: two involved people

Let us consider the situation of an AA couple, which in

Handy's survey was the second most common mix after the BD pattern. With two As, both are ambitious, and both are also caring and co-operative. Friends tend to be common, activities joint; life is hectic, intense, involved. Both partners will get involved with housework, cooking or (where applicable) looking after the children. Generally, both partners have been to university or college and discussion at mealtimes is likely to be about both work and ideas (in contrast with BD couples, where meal conversations revolve around events or things that need doing). AA relationships are equal partnerships: your friends would find it hard to say which of you was the more dominant.

If you are in an AA mode the problem is likely to be one of capacity, or time, for each of you to fulfil your professional objectives, and still have a full and rewarding home life. This problem is particularly acute where both partners are required to travel extensively in the course of their work. Two of my most amusing friends, Chris and Andy (who is a she), are always travelling all over the globe to different places in the course of their work: they have two children, aged 9 and 11, a demanding dog, and two large houses to look after as well. They are both genuinely involved in running the household. Their friends are nearly all mutual friends. Recently Chris had to vacation in Mexico in order to see Andy, whose work took her out there for a month, and their children, who went with her. It seems to work, largely because they can afford and choose to employ an au pair, a cleaner and a gardener, but sometimes I am concerned about the stress imposed by the different demands on their time.

The AA pattern: possible strains from your new job

If you are in an AA relationship and starting a new job, the question you have to ask is whether the demands on your time and the travel content will be substantially more than in your previous job. If so, whether you realise it or not, you may end up loading your partner with a more than fair share of the domestic workload, and you may also find yourself being excluded (because of lack of time) from a lot of the 'involved' activities from which you currently derive a lot of pleasure.

You may be able to keep the strains within acceptable limits by being sensitive to the dangers, and by avoiding the extremes of time and travel commitment. All ambitious and hard-working people are fair game for the puritan ethic trap, where we measure commitment and achievement by the inputs of time or discomfort. Most people could achieve as much as they do currently, or more, by cutting their own working hours by 30 per cent, organising themselves better (or getting an assistant to do this) and delegating more. Equally, most people never get round to doing this. It requires a conscious element of willpower and self-discipline, paradoxically, to work less hard. Focus on outputs, not inputs. Analyse what you do over a week and work out what could have been delegated, without loss of quality or impact. You will be surprised what can be done or not done. Do not feel guilty if you enjoy life more, as long as you are effective.

It is the same with travel. With modern communications (phone, fax, computer links, voice communications, phone-conferencing, video-conferencing) there is a much reduced need to dash around the country or the world, taking a weary body and mind to depths of unproductiveness that would never be plumbed in your office. Do not travel just because it has always been thus. Ask if it is really necessary or, even if pressing the flesh is essential, whether someone else could not do it. See if you can persuade the person you planned to visit to come to you. Unless you really enjoy travelling for its own sake (and if you do, you are probably a B rather than an A), aim to cut it down dramatically, and only change your intentions if you are convinced that your professional effectiveness is being diminished as a result of less frequent travel.

Playing portfolio relationships: moving from AA to BD?

You may be able to keep the AA relationship happily afloat by adopting these wise moves. But if your move to a more demanding job coincides with, or is followed by, a change in domestic circumstances (usually the arrival of children and/or the move to a larger house in a more remote location), or by your partner landing a much more demanding job, there will be a need to review the AA pattern and its sustainability. You may need to move to a BD pattern, which would require one partner to give up his or her career (for a time) in order to look after the home front and provide support to the other in his or her job. This should only be undertaken if both partners are happy with the move and realise the sacrifices being made by each other (because, inevitably, the person who stays in demanding, full-time employment will regret the loss of 'home market share', just as the other partner will miss certain aspects of their career). Wherever possible, the person putting his or her career temporarily on hold should actively keep open the option of a later return to it, and should also take a challenging part-time job, paid or unpaid.

Another option for AA partners with more demanding jobs that they can happily accommodate is to switch to the BB pattern. Let us first review this in its own terms.

The BB pattern: dual income thrusters

The natural BB pattern is of two thrusters, eager to get ahead in their careers, with few caring/supportive instincts and a high need for independence. These relationships are characterised by friendly (and sometimes unfriendly) competition, high earnings, high expenditure and a limiting of domestic commitments. The BB pattern is much easier to make work without children. One interesting example of the modern BB pattern is a gay professional couple, both with demanding and well-paid jobs, each with their separate leisure interests. Robin is a successful and rising PR executive; Simon an equally successful accountant. They both work over 70 hours a week and are often out of town. In the evenings when they are together they almost always go out for a meal, or order food in while they each work or read separately. They each have their own circle of friends and preferred recreations. The relationship may seem minimalist to many but it works well. There are also many examples of successful BB marriages, though only a minority of these have children.

BB patterns that work well rely very heavily on outside services that minimise the extent of housework. BB couples neither have the time nor inclination for this, so are often surrounded by an army of contract workers that in a different age would have been called servants. BBs have cleaners, nannies, au pairs, gardeners, drivers, housekeepers, caterers, interior designers, housesitters and personal assistants. They are great patrons of restaurants and hotels. They hold several credit cards. When they have to eat in, they get someone else to cook or, if times are hard, fall back on a high-quality convenience food. Consequently, although they earn a great deal, BBs are not generally great savers.

The BB pattern tends to cope well with the extra stress arising from one (or even both) partner(s) getting a more demanding job. Since the relationship already works with limited time together, and since the household is deliberately made relatively undemanding, a further accentuation of these trends need not cause major problems. It can, however, go too far, particularly if one of the partners is not a wholehearted B and has a strong admixture of A characteristics (a wish to be involved). In these circumstances, if strains arise, the partners need to reassess the work requirements they each have, and find a way of limiting the time and travel required of one or both of them, in the way suggested above for the AAs.

Moving from AA to BB?

For AAs under strain, particularly if there are B elements in either or both partners, and if the shift to a BD pattern is not acceptable, the option of moving to a BB pattern should be considered. In practice this means retaining the equality of the relationship by reducing the commitment to housework and related 'involved' activities for both parties. This requires either reduced home commitments (for example, moving from a larger country home to a smaller town one, nearer work; or agreeing that grown-up children should leave home), or much greater use of family or paid help with homowork, or both. A move to a BB pattern means that for a stretch of your lives together you will be both placing a higher priority of career. If you make this move you should set a likely timescale for this, discuss which pattern you might move to at the end of this time and also set a review date (perhaps a year from now) to see whether the new pattern is working.

The CC partnership: two loners

This is a relationship between two relatively unambitious individuals of similar background, age and temperament who are self-sufficient, and want to be left in peace to pursue their own private interests. There is relatively little communal activity or discussion in such households. The two partners often have different friends and sometimes take their holidays separately: this is not a reaction to conflict, but the natural pattern for contentment in the relationship. If you are in this category, the demands from your new job are unlikely to create a problem at home in the short term. The only danger is that in the medium to long term you will drift further apart from your partner, so that one of you ends the relationship.

The AB pattern: lop-sided thrusting

This is quite an interesting relationship, where both partners are serious about their careers, but one wishes to be involved and supportive, and the other prefers to do his or her own thing. Conflict can arise in such relationships, because the A wants the B to be more involved in social or mutual activities – giving dinner parties, meeting friends or just doing things together – while the B is always wanting to sneak out to pursue a private interest, or be left alone to read or watch TV. What also tends to happen is that the A ends up doing a more than a fair share of the housework, which he or she likes and places higher priority on than the partner, but this may cause conflict if the A feels that his or her career is not advancing as it should, as a result of having to do more housework.

If you are the A in an AB relationship, your new job may exacerbate this tension. The best way to deal with this is to be realistic about the time commitments of your new job and to have an explicit discussion with your partner, agreeing if necessary for him or her to take on some of your housework responsibilities. If this does not appear realistic or fails to work in practice, you may need to shift towards the BB pattern for a time, and the same considerations will apply as for an AA couple moving to BB (see Moving from AA to BB, above).

If you are the B with an A partner, your new job may serve as an excuse for you to do even less housework and spend less time with your partner. Although this may seem convenient to you, it is really a trap for your relationship. If you value it, take the following steps:

- limit your extra time and travel commitments (see The AA pattern, above);
- try to be more social with the time you do have at home;
- spend money on contracting out the less interesting home duties so that your A partner is not unduly burdened.

AC: one involved careerist and one loner

Frankly, this is an odd couple. Such relationships are rare and either do not last or, if they do, they do so against all the rules and every particle of common sense, because of the perverse strength of affection between the partners. The time pressure on the A in the relationship is intense: he or she is the breadwinner, homemaker and social co-ordinator, whose ambition, family and social endeavours are not likely to be fully appreciated by the partner, who is both less ambitious and less involved.

If you are the A in an AC relationship, your new job will raise the time pressure still further. You should certainly aim to contract out the 'bottom half' of housework wherever possible, reduce the amount of housework and try to 'delegate' some of it to your partner. In effect, you will then be moving to much more of a BC relationship.

BC: one thruster and one loner

In its natural, original form, both parties have a high drive for autonomy, but only one is an ambitious careerist and the C partner more often than not does not have a full-time job. This combination can make sense, although, as with the CC duo, there is always a risk of drifting further and further apart. Home commitments will sometimes be quite minimal and individual interests pursued.

The BC combo is relatively impervious to increased work commitments from either side, although it would be wise for you to spend more time together on common activities to avoid drifting out of your relationship and the matrix altogether.

The AD combo: one involved, one carer

This is another relationship that tends to work well, although it is not as frequent as might be expected. Both people are the helping and supporting type, but only one has a strong need to achieve and be dominant. Frequently the D partner looks after the home and has at most a part-time job, although the A will try to participate in looking after any children as far as time permits.

Increased job commitments for the A will cause only minor problems, because both parties will naturally want to avoid any deterioration in the quality of domestic life and will take intelligent steps accordingly.

In the unusual case of the D partner having a new and

more demanding job, this should herald a move in the short or medium term to the AA pattern, with a more equal split of home responsibilities. The A will need to be sensitive to this and allocate more time to housework.

The CD relationship: one loner and one carer

In the CD household, the D (Carer) is usually the person who runs the household and the C (Loner) the person who pursues his or her own interests. Not many readers of this book are likely to be in the CD pattern, since the priority to career is low in both cases.

If the C starts a new and challenging job, the C should move towards B behaviour, resulting in the BD pattern, which is perfectly viable and should not present any major problems. If anything, it should improve the quality of the relationship.

But if the D (Carer) is promoted into a much more demanding job, there is likely to be high stress on the D, which may be unnoticed or come as a surprise to the C (Loner). The D will either give inappropriately low commitment to the job, or the home will suffer, or both. To ensure appropriate behaviour at work and home, the pattern must shift, but this is difficult. The D could move to being an A, but if the C still behaved in the same way this would not improve matters much, since the AC relationship is not a natural fit. The best move from a work perspective is probably to go for the BC pattern, which is viable, but only if home commitments can be reduced or contracted out without reducing the quality of home life, on which the D (rightly) places high priority. Another option would be to try to move the C towards behaving as a D, resulting in the viable AD pattern. The trouble is that most Cs are not flexible enough to assume D's housework responsibilities with a willing heart. This case will require careful discussion between the partners.

The DD relationship: two carers

This is another pattern which is perfectly viable as a relationship, but rather unusual for someone taking on a serious new job. The D who undertakes this will only do so satisfactorily by moving towards the A (Involved: Supportive but Ambitious) quadrant. This would then lead to the AD pattern, which should work well enough. The result will be that the previously equal split of housework will move more towards the residual D (that is, the person who does not have the demanding new job), but provided both parties are prepared for this it should be fine.

To conclude . . .

By now you should know which relationship pattern you are currently in, whether there are likely to be relationship problems arising from your new job and, if so, what solutions are available. You should now have secured the home base. Now is the time to move on, and consider your exciting and exacting new work environment.

But before you do that, I have a little test for you, a pattern you should get used to. At the end of each chapter of this book you will find a checklist to help you to measure how well you have prepared for each part of the journey. Do not proceed to the next stage until you pass the test! Good luck with it.

First day zero checklist

(To be filled in before you start your new job)

1 Do you know which of the ten relationship patterns you are in? *Tick*

A Yes ☐

B No/Not sure ☐

2 Have you discussed the pattern with your partner?

A Yes ☐

B No ☐

3 Have you thought seriously about the home impact of your new job?

A Yes ☐

B No/Not yet ☐

4 Have you agreed with your partner any necessary changes in your relationship pattern and your home life?

A Yes ☐

B No/Not yet ☐

5 Are you confident that you can handle more onerous work requirements, and also the demands necessary to sustain a good relationship and home life?

A Yes ☐

B No ☐

C Not sure, but I am working on it ☐

SCORING YOUR ANSWERS

Score 20 for **each** A answer, 0 for **each** B, and 10 for the C. Add up the total.

INTERPRETING YOUR SCORES

90–100 Well done! Go on to the next chapter.

60–80 Persevere. You are clearly taking this seriously, but you need to fill in the gaps until you reach a score of 90 or 100 before moving on to the next chapter. You need to feel confident about the home base before you can give your undivided attention to the work context, which is the subject of the rest of the book.

0–50 Hmm. Sorry, but you ought to read this chapter again and act on it before proceeding. Only skip this chapter if you have no relationship or place little value on it.

2

Before you begin: work

A walk on the quiet side

Some new bosses start planning what to do in their new job on day one. Too early, you may think. Well, you would be wrong. It is far too late, actually.

If you don't walk into your new empire with at least a rough idea of what you want to achieve, what the main things going for you are, and what are the main obstacles you are likely to encounter, you will get knocked on the head by unreasonable reality before you get into your stride. Then it will be too late to plan: there will never be time to get round to it; and you will be at the mercy of circumstances.

And working out what you want to do, before you arrive, will take time and introspection. Since it's difficult to do this when you are still in your old job, it is a good idea to take a holiday – and as long a holiday as you can – between jobs.

If you can't take a holiday, set aside quality, uninterrupted time in the evenings or weekends to think things through, weeks or months ahead of the start date for the new job. Go for a walk in the woods or the mountains, discuss the issues with your partner and/or a trusted friend who is not in the company, or do whatever

helps you to relax and think. Write it down if this helps, or keep it in your head: do whatever works better for you.

Assess the terrain

Before you go off walking (or whatever), gather as much intelligence on your new territory and people as you can discreetly do. If you are new to the company or unit, talk to all of your friends and acquaintances who are in it or know about it. If it's a new company, send off for the annual report. Read all publicity and press reports you can lay your hands on. When talking about it, don't just ask the obvious questions, but try to find out what sort of people and culture the firm has.

If you are new to the industry, get up to speed on the basic facts and buzzwords before you arrive. Buy or borrow any necessary books and ask the company itself to supply any reading matter it considers relevant.

Even if you are already working in the unit or company, the terrain as boss will be different and needs thinking about. The best starting point is to think about how far you will need or want to change things. So reflect on the current incumbent boss's objectives, approach and style, the team's performance and output, the unit's reputation inside the firm and/or the firm's reputation outside with customers, suppliers, competitors and the local community.

Spot the extent and source of competitive success

How successful is the unit or firm? Has its output been growing or declining, both in volume and in value? Have

competitors been growing faster: and if so, who and why? Does the successful competitor provide a product at a lower price (and therefore probably a lower cost)? Does the successful competitor provide a better service or quality and get paid more for it? Or has the successful competitor found a special type of customer where it can provide exactly what is needed and get well rewarded for that?

You may not be able to answer these questions fully, but at least you should start thinking about them and develop some ideas or theories about them.

These questions about competitive position – that is, why a unit or company is able to exist and prosper – apply not just to whole companies or to commercial corporations, but equally to units within companies, to cost centres, to charities, social services and any type or organisation. Why is the unit there? Whatever it does, there will be actual or theoretical alternatives to it, other ways that the output is or could be generated. Why should it be done within your unit?

The answer to these questions will be found among the following:

- **cost/price**, that is, the unit can perform the service cheaper or more efficiently than alternatives
- **quality**, that is, the unit delivers a better product or service than others do or could
- **service**, that is, the unit is more responsive to the people who use the service than alternative providers, and delivers the service quicker, more reliably or with greater warmth
- **natural protected position**, where, because of some expertise, wealth, location, technology or other real factor, others simply cannot provide the product or service

- **unnatural protected position, or historical accident**, where, because of a cartel, government decree, professional restrictive practice, force of circumstance or tradition, or simple ignorance or inertia, others who could in theory provide the product or service are prevented from doing so.

Assess the extent and mix of your unit's competitive advantage. Then think about how sustainable it is and what changes in the environment or actions by others could upset the applecart. How safe is it to continue with your unit's operations pretty much as they are? What could be done relatively easily to reinforce or create competitive advantage? In particular, if the bulk of the unit's current advantage falls into the last category, what could be done to create a natural advantage (in any of the earlier categories)? A natural advantage based on economics or customer appeal is a much sounder and more satisfying basis for existing than artificial restrictions, as bureaucracies, government companies and unions around the world are discovering.

Are the people a team?

Find out all you can about your prospective staff. If it is a large group, concentrate on the most senior people, but also on a few of the younger possible high fliers. If it is a small group, find out about them all.

Does the group currently operate as an effective team? If not, why not? What is the current boss's leadership style: laid back, dictatorial, charismatic or inconsistent? Is the leader effective or ineffective? Is he or she loved, tolerated or hated? Remember that these are separate dimensions, as shown below: a popular leader can be ineffective, or an unpopular one effective, as well as the two other options.

The leadership quadrants

	POPULAR	UNPOPULAR
EFFECTIVE	1	2
INEFFECTIVE	3	4

Think about yourself and your leadership style

In Chapter 5 we will take an intensive look at your management style and personal characteristics. The main point to be aware of here is that leadership comes in all shapes and sizes, and you should select the leadership vestments that fit your body and soul best. Then think about how you and the team are likely to interact.

This is potentially dangerous ground. Over time, most managers select and shape their team according to their own attributes. Moshe Dayan is reported to have said that the greatest general is the person who can use ordinary troops to best effect. It is interesting that intelligence bears only a slight correlation to success in life, whether measured by wealth, happiness or any other criterion. A determined and effective team of very ordinary people can usually outperform a collection of much more intelligent but indolent individuals. It is also true that most managers consciously or unconsciously attract and reward the sort of people who can reinforce their own effectiveness or correct their weaknesses, thus making themselves and the team more successful than they would otherwise be.

This option is not normally available, at first, to the new boss. Instead, you are going to inherit a team moulded to suit the personality and abilities of the current boss, who may be very different from you. There will almost certainly be an instant and in-built mismatch between the team you will have, on the one hand, and, on the other, the team you could make most effective and which would make you most effective. Paradoxically, therefore, you may be a better boss than your predecessor, and yet, at first, you and the team may perform less well than before. This disadvantage can be reversed over time: but not unless you realise it and even then not very quickly.

The wise new boss therefore adopts a management style which is half-way between your natural style and that which belonged to your predecessor (assuming that he or she had been reasonably effective). Gradually, as you change the team's behaviour and composition, you can then revert to your natural style.

You will also, in time, be able to change the nature of your job and your unit's role in life to play to your own strengths, and to the collective strength that you can liberate within the team. You will shift the competitive advantage of the team, so you should therefore seek those arenas of activity which will most reward the team's skills.

At the outset, however, you should realise the limitations

imposed on you by the team's way of working and the leadership style of your predecessor.

How much change is necessary?

Do you want to keep things just as they are? This is most unlikely! If not, what are the most important changes you would like to introduce? How likely would you be to succeed in each of these and how long would each one take to achieve?

Assess the need for change and the speed at which it can safely proceed in the light of your reflections on the previous three sections: the unit's competitive advantage; the nature of the team; and your leadership style contrasted with that of your predecessor.

If all appears to be going reasonably well, there is real competitive advantage, there is a genuine team operating, and your predecessor was an effective and popular leader, it will be sensible to make very few changes at first, even if your own style and abilities could make major leaps forward possible. There will be plenty of time for this in the future. The key thing when you begin in the position will be to avoid any impression that you are less effective than your predecessor (which, for the reasons explained above, you probably will be). 'If it ain't broke, don't fix it'; emphasise continuity, and make your changes gradually and with guile.

If there is a weak or eroding competitive position, but no imminent crisis, and the team and leadership has apparently been operating reasonably effectively (but with a poor strategy), you will need to make changes before long, but again you should be cautious in not shifting the team's way of working too radically or abruptly. You will need to check that your diagnosis is correct before acting, and then you will need to convince the team or certain key individuals that change is necessary.

If there is serious and immediate competitive weakness, and a crisis is looming, you will need to make changes quickly and radically. Likewise, whatever the competitive position, if the leadership has been unpopular and ineffective, you can make your changes at once and with as much fanfare as suits your style.

If you decide to opt for radical, immediate change, it will be important to define your 'Cause' in broad terms, to communicate this to the team. The Cause could be improved quality and service, lower costs, an attack on bureaucracy, higher volume and market share, or whatever you consider appropriate. The Cause should not be too precise, both because your knowledge will be quite imperfect at the start, and because you will alienate too many of your people if you appear to know it all and be telling them in detail how they can do better. Wherever possible, the cause should reflect genuine concerns that the team already has, but which your predecessor ignored or suppressed. This is true even where the team's concerns may be only slightly related to the underlying competitive weakness: incorporating the team's worries and melding them with the real weakness is a politic step.

You should know your cause, if there is to be one, before you start the job. You can refine it later.

Target your key allies

You will need a lot of help when you arrive. Before you

start, therefore, work out where it can come from. Genuine allies must be differentiated from apparent allies, who will offer the fabled 'all help short of useful assistance'. Allies fall into five major categories, as follows:

1 BOSSES

Your boss, and perhaps his or her boss, was/were responsible for appointing you. How far they will help will depend on the extent of their personal commitment to you, their understanding of the need for change, their sympathy with your cause, and their personality and general risk profile. Work out how far it is worth lobbying for their support, when to do this and how much actual assistance they can give.

2 STAFF

You may know some of the team already, and be able to count on a degree of support and intelligence from these individuals. On top of this, key team members may appreciate the need for change. Work out as quickly as you can who these people are and what they can contribute.

3 NEWCOMERS

By newcomers is meant your own people whom you appoint. Sometimes you can insist on going into a new job with one or more lieutenant(s) whom you know and trust, and with whom you work well. The value of this cannot be overestimated. If major change is necessary and you cannot get newcomers in simultaneously with your arrival, plan to move heaven and earth to get appropriate 'own people' installed as soon as possible thereafter.

4 INTRA-FIRM

People in other departments (usually the heads) will have a vested interest in your department improving its performance. Try to meet them and assess their attitudes before you arrive.

5 CUSTOMERS

If change is necessary, your customers will probably realise it and be demanding it (one way or another) already. Visit large or dissatisfied customers as soon as you can and take a verbatim note of their wishes so you can convey this to your people (and perhaps to your bosses).

Decide your first actions

Your first 'spontaneous' actions should be carefully planned and scripted. Since actions speak far louder than words, work out what your symbolic first actions are going to be. These may be the time at which you arrive or leave work, the questions you ask, the people you see, how you spend your time (for instance, with customers, or wandering around on the shopfloor, rather than in the executive suite with the door shut), the actions of others that you praise, or the way you spend or avoid spending money.

When Alan Jackson took over from Sir Owen Green at BTR, the first thing he did, to symbolise his commitment to maintaining the low cost culture of BTR, was to take a company car that already had 100 000 miles on the clock. The action was noted and approved.

If you have a flair for the dramatic, make sure that the gesture is symbolically sound and reflects your Cause.

Start behaving as the new boss should

Before you arrive, and as early as possible, start behaving as you would when in your new role. This is most effective if your new position is in the same company, but even if it is not, start feeling your way into the new role, so that it will seem natural when you arrive.

This is a most effective gambit when you know about your promotion weeks or preferably months in advance of nearly everyone else in the firm. Wise superbosses usually tell prospective new bosses about their planned promotion well in advance, so that the boss-designate can begin to display the skills and perspective appropriate to the new role before the promotion is announced to everyone else. The promotion then appears natural and just, when it is announced.

If you are going from a functional role (such as sales or manufacturing) to a general management role, start to adopt a generalist approach rather than the narrow one which your function would naturally lead you to. If you are going from a technical job in research to a marketing position, or vice versa, bone up on the new area of expertise before your promotion is announced, so that your new colleagues will not think that you are functionally ignorant.

Map out your 100-day plan

After reading the whole book, map out what you hope to achieve in your first 100 days. Then set objective tests for yourself, so that you will know whether and when you have passed these milestones. Try to keep the objectives as simple as possible, so you can remember them in your mind without having to look them up. If you need a paper record to remind you, keep it in a Filofax or other binder which you can carry round with you and consult at any time.

How well have you done?

If you have done all this before arriving, you will have hugely increased your chances of success. If you haven't, it may be difficult to recover.

The second day zero checklist

(To be filled in immediately before you start as the new boss)

1 How much time have you spent reflecting on your new job?

Tick

A Have taken a holiday of at least ten days, and reflected extensively in the evenings/weekends ☐

B Have taken a holiday of four to nine days, and reflected extensively at evenings/weekends ☐

C Have reflected extensively at evenings/weekends ☐

D If I am honest, I have been too busy to spend much time reflecting ☐

2 Do you feel prepared to start, in that you think you understand most of the pitfalls awaiting you?

A Yes, probably ☐

B To some degree ☐

C Not really ☐

3 Do you believe you have at least a basic understanding of the company's business activities, markets and technology?

A Yes ☐

B Not sure ☐

C No ☐

4 Do you believe you have some idea about the company (and unit's) culture, values and ways of working?

A Yes ☐

B Not sure ☐

C No ☐

5 What is the company or unit's main source of competitive advantage?

A Cost/Price ☐

B Quality ☐

C Service ☐

D Natural protected position ☐

E Unnatural protected position/historical accident ☐

F Some other characteristic (define it) ☐

G I don't know ☐

6 Can you summarise the outgoing boss's management style with reasonable confidence in one sentence?

A Yes (do so!) ☐

B No ☐

7 Can you summarise the differences between the management style of the outgoing boss and your natural management style in one sentence?

A Yes (Again, do so!) ☐

B No ☐

8 Do you plan to modify your natural management style initially to make it more similar to that of your predecessor?

A No, that would be the wrong thing to do ☐

B Yes, totally ☐

C Yes, to some degree ☐

D No, it is unnecessary as we both have similar styles ☐

9 How much change is necessary in the way the unit or company you are taking over is run?

A Very little ☐

B Quite a lot ☐

C A great deal ☐

D I don't know; I will only know after being there for a few months ☐

10 Do you know who your key allies will be?

A No, it's too early to tell ☐

B Yes, pretty much ☐

C Yes, some of them ☐

D I don't really need allies if I do what I think is right and what the unit/company needs ☐

11 Do you know what your first actions will be?

A That depends on what I find when I arrive ☐

B Yes, I will emphasise that it is business as usual ☐

C Yes, I will make a few symbolic gestures to indicate my cause and values ☐

D No ☐

12 Have you already started behaving as you will when you start as the new boss?

A No, that would be inappropriate until I am in the saddle and have the power and legitimacy of my new role ☐

B No, that would be silly as the job is in a different company ☐

C Yes, to some degree ☐

13 Have you made your 100-day plan yet?

A I will wait until I have arrived before doing that, but will do it in the first week ☐

B Yes, though it will need modification later ☐

C Yes, and I shall stick to it through thick and thin ☐

D Such a plan is unnecessary; I am a pragmatist and will take things as they come ☐

SCORING YOUR ANSWERS

Question 1

For A, score 20 points
For B, score 15 points
For C, score 10 points
For D, score 0

Questions 2–4

For **each** A, score 10 points
For **each** B, score 5 points
For **each** C, score 0

Question 5

For A to F, score 10 points
For G, score 0

Questions 6 to 7

For **each** A, score 10
For **each** B, score 0

Question 8
For A, score 0
For B, score 0
For C, score 10
For D, score 10

Question 9
For A, B or C, score 10
For D, score 0

Question 10
For A, score 0
For B or C, score 10
For D, score 0

Question 11
For A or B, score 0
For C, score 10
For D, score 0

Question 12
For A, score 0
For B, score 5
For C, score 10

Question 13
For A, score 0
For B, score 10
For C or D, score 0

INTERPRETING YOUR SCORES

115–140 points You are well prepared and should look forward to your first week.

70–110 points You have thought about some of the issues but there are still a large number of gaps and uncertainties, and you will probably have a difficult first week. If at all possible, defer your start for a week and reflect some more.

0–65 points You are either very honest or have not yet read this book! Read or reread the book, and for your sake defer the start of your job, or else you will be at the mercy of circumstances and quite likely to fail in the new job.

3

The first ten days

Expect the first ten days to be both fascinating and frightening. Don't worry when the unexpected happens; maintain whatever is your natural style, but also try to exude a calm confidence. Meanwhile, you should be quietly gathering data and getting your bearings.

There are three sets of questions to answer, related to:

- the people you lead
- the mission of your company or unit
- the competitive position of your company or unit.

Your people

You should spend at least half of your first ten days talking to the people you lead: to all of your direct reports and a sprinkling of people further down in the organisation if they report ultimately to you.

Talk to your direct reports individually. You should look both for relevant information about the way the unit works, its markets, technology and contacts, and also for insight about the person, and his or her attitudes and aspirations. At the back of your mind, you should be assessing each individual on two dimensions: his or her competence, and his or her attitude towards you and the rest of the team. Mentally, or with the help of a piece of paper, you should classify each person on these two dimensions, as shown below:

Attitude and competence quadrants

ATTITUDE	COMPETENCE: High	COMPETENCE: Low
Positive	1	2
Negative	3	4

The best result is clearly if someone falls into quadrant 1: is competent and supportive of you and the team. That is, the person has a positive attitude towards the unit and your leadership.

Some people, however, may fall into one of the other three quadrants of the box. For someone in box 2, you will need to find a way of improving competence, either by changing the nature of the job to fit more with the person's natural skills, or by training and counselling. This is a medium-term objective and does not have to be done right away.

An individual in box 3, with high competence but a negative attitude, will need more immediate attention. Such a person could cause considerable damage to you before you realise it. You need to change his or her attitude quickly, or else remove them to another unit or organisation not under your leadership. The first is the better solution, since you will then have the individual's talents at your disposal, but you need to be pragmatic and, if the second is more easily attainable (which is often the case), go for it.

The most serious cause of a new boss's neutering, and consequent failure, is failure to recognise or deal with box 3 people. Diagnosis of the disease, and a decision on whether to reform or remove the individual, must be made within the first ten days and successfully implemented within the first month. Few of us like to believe that we have deadly enemies, and even fewer like to engage in confrontation, so we tend to shut our eyes to political sabotage or passive resistance, especially from the ablest people. There can be no more serious mistake for the new boss. If you do nothing else in the first two weeks, you must identify any box 3 people, and form a plan to deal with them.

People in box 4 present less of a dilemma. They are less potentially helpful than box 3 people (with changed attitude) and also less dangerous. Nevertheless, you cannot allow your team to include any box 4 people for any length of time. Present the individuals with your perceptions and with a plan to improve their competence, but make your help to achieve this conditional on a change in attitude. If this is not forthcoming, make plans to 'export' such people as soon as possible.

By the end of 100 days, the successful new boss will only have box 1 direct reports. Will you be one of these successes?

Questions to ask your people

Of course, the best way to assess your people is to do it as a by-product of finding out about what they do and gathering information about your new domain. The questions to ask should be pretty evident to you, but should probably include the following:

- What do you do and why?
- Who and what do you depend on to do a good job?
- What would enable you to do a better job?
- Are there things you do that could be done more quickly, or not all, with little or no loss of value?
- What would you like to spend more time doing, and how would this help the team and our customers?
- Are you fully stretched?
- Could some of the things you do be delegated to a lower cost resource without serious loss of quality?
- How can you best help me to help the team/what can you do to help the transition to a new boss (me!)?
- If you were in my position, what other steps would you take to improve the team's overall performance and morale?
- How can we make this team one of the best in the company/the industry?
- Is there anything else you and I should discuss right now?

Mission

'Mission' is one of those grand sounding words that many

use, but few understand or care about passionately. You should be one of the few. Work will not be fun for you or your team unless you believe in what you do. To believe in what you do, you need to articulate what this is, and it has to be something worthwhile, and something which goes beyond the purely self-interested motives of the team.

Successful companies and units must have a purpose or role that justifies their existence. They must in some way be a force for good. They must be better than their run of the mill equivalents: which is why they have above average success. This cannot be defined purely in financial terms, since profit is a result of doing things well (assuredly, a very important result), not the cause.

John F. Kennedy said, 'Ask not what your country can do for you, but what you can do for your country.' The same principle should apply to your team. Each unit should be asking itself what it can do for its organisation. Each organisation should be asking what it can do for the world. The team should then take pride in, and derive inspiration from, executing its mission for the benefit of others.

This may sound very idealistic and high flown, but at root it is just common sense. The most satisfying thing in the world is to be useful to others and acknowledged for the contribution made. So you need to decide where lies your team's 'mission' to the organisation and beyond. You may decide that this is something pretty humble. This is no matter, as long as it is real and of value. The tone of a company is often set by seemingly trivial things, done well or badly. Are the telephones answered within three rings? Are receptionists friendly? Is the architecture warm and human or harsh and forbidding (this dimension is entirely independent of cost)? Does the internal mail system work properly? Is the salesforce good at feeding back customer needs to manufacturing and research? Is respect for the individual a hallmark of the organisation? What about respect for the environment and service of the local community?

At the level of the company as a whole, where is its distinctive contribution to the world? What can it do better than others? Can it invent new products, provide the best service to a particular group of customers, upgrade the standards of ordinary consumers? Provide fun by being more creative? Provide the lowest cost solution?

Some companies already have a real sense of mission, but 80 per cent do not. Creating a genuine and long-lasting mission where none exists takes years for a company, and is often the result of bottom-up evolution. From your standpoint as a new boss, you should be concerned with your own team and its mission. If the company of which you are a part already has a real sense of mission, try to define your unit's role to fit in with and reinforce the corporate mission. If the company does not have an overall sense of mission, try to create an example in your own unit of how having a sense of purpose and service to others can made work more fun and more productive. Make sure the team has a sense of collective identity and purpose, and that it takes pride in it.

Your team's competitive position

You will recall that we discussed in Chapter 2 the competitive advantage of your unit or company. This is part of the 'Mission' as discussed above, but is the more narrowly commercial rationale, that is, the reason why you can be more profitable or more efficient than your competitors (similar units or companies).

Now you are on the inside, you should refine or change your view about the unit's competitive advantage. At this stage, be content to gather data and opinions in the team, but be thinking all the time about whether the advantage is good enough and how to improve it.

Reflections on mission and competitive position, together with your chats with the team, should lead you either to modify your Cause (the broad change you wish to introduce), or to feel increased confidence that it is appropriate. We will discuss below how far and when your reflections should be shared with the team as a whole.

How assertive should you be?

One of the most crucial and difficult early decisions is how assertive you should be in the first few days. Should you be open about your early impressions and thoughts, in order to minimise misunderstandings and start to generate change? Or should you bide your time, give few hostages to fortune and wait until you are sure of your ground?

As with all important decisions in life, there is no infallibly correct prescription. You must use your own common sense and judgement. But two hints may help you here.

First, there is your own personality. Attempts to cloak or constrain your own personality may increase your effectiveness at critical times, but all things being equal you will be more effective if you behave naturally. If you are naturally assertive, explain that you are, but make it clear when you are thinking aloud and when you are laying down the law. If you are naturally more reserved or introspective, adhere to this style most of the time, but force yourself to be clear and assertive on those few occasions that require it (such as when you are dealing with Box 3 people).

Second, take account of the extent of change necessary. If you have inherited a unit which is inefficient or performing poorly, you should be soberly assertive, even if this cuts across your natural style. Conversely, if the unit is doing well and little immediate change is required, but you are a natural extrovert, you should tone down your natural assertiveness in the early days, lest casual comments set off an avalanche of unnecessary change.

How to deal with difficult team members

Most of your people will be relatively straightforward and co-operative. But how do you deal with the idle, the obstructive, the secretly subversive, the crawlers and the insouciants?

Here are some general hints on dealing with all these people.

- **Remember your classifications into the attitude/competence boxes.** By definition, these people will be in box 3 or box 4. Deal with the box 3 (competent but negative) people more urgently, because they have both more upside and downside for you and the team than the box 4 people.
- **See the good as well as the bad.** Praise whatever good characteristics you can find in these people, including occasions on which they inconsistently display skill or positive attitudes. If you praise someone for something, they will usually try to live up to it.
- **Stress the good of the team as a whole.** Your job is to

help the team, not to advance your own career. So try not to say, 'This is how I want it', or 'This is how it must be'. Rather, ask questions which take it for granted that everyone must want the good of the overall team, like 'Don't you think the team would be more effective if you did X rather than Y?' or 'Couldn't you help A and B [team members] better if you did things this way?', or make assertions like, 'We need your help in doing Z if the team is to deliver our objective of W'.

- **Secure agreement to actions that can be monitored.** Do not end a chat without getting agreement that behaviour will be changed in specific ways that can be monitored easily to see whether change has occurred. Then ensure that you know whether it has and give positive or negative feedback. Psychologists tell us that it is often easier to change attitudes by changing behaviour than the other way round (the way we in the West think of first). Concentrate on small battles for action.
- **Use the team as a whole to help you put pressure on recalcitrant individuals.** Wherever possible, get peer pressure applied naturally.
- **Do not dissimulate.** When someone's actions or approach are unacceptable to you, do not string them along or fail to express (politely) the full force of your feeling. It is amazing how often we all tend to do this, whether because we need the person's technical skill, or because we are unsure of our political ground, or simply because we shrink from unpleasant confrontations. Do not fall into these traps; you will only make things worse, as well as simply deferring the day when the nettle will have to be grasped.
- **Do not compromise.** If something is wrong, it is wrong. Persevere until the solution is found. Your team

will respect your resolution.

Second, here are some hints on dealing with particular categories of difficult people:

- **Mr Idle.** If the only problem is lack of industry, this is relatively easily dealt with. Pair Mr Idle up with someone who is highly productive, but of the same ability level, and ensure that their comparative outputs are highly visible. If this doesn't work, be very direct with the person, but take the view that the fault is relatively easily corrected. If it isn't, the person must go on to the transfer list.
- **Ms Obstructive.** This is someone who is openly hostile to your plans for change. Try the gambits in the general hints above, especially emphasising the good of the team as a whole. Deal with any points of logic fairly and dispassionately. If you disagree because of opinions about matters of fact, try to get the data gathered to settle the issue. Try to assume that the person involved must have your positive attitude to life, rather than the negative attitude she displays. Avoid injecting personal antagonism or reciprocating personal hostility. But at the end of the day, make it clear that, unless Ms Obstructive can prove that her way is better for the team as a whole than your way, no amount of obstruction will succeed. A smart Ms Obstructive will then see the light. The less intelligent variety can be consigned to the dustbin of history.
- **Mr Secretly-Subversive.** A more dangerous variant of his cousin Ms Obstructive: someone who says Yes but acts No. The acting can take the form of direct countermanding of your instructions or of passive resistance (i.e. not taking the action required). In either case, detection is the first priority. Once detected, you

must confront Mr S-S and make it clear this is unacceptable behaviour. If it happens more than once, Mr S-S must go to the top of the transfer list.

- **Mrs Crawler.** An embarrassment rather than a danger, but one who is best openly discouraged. Explain your inherent modesty and aversion to extravagant praise. If she does not take the hint, ensure that her duties take her as far away as possible from yours.
- **Mr Insouciant.** This is someone who may be pleasant and supportive, but who lives in a world of his own, is unaware of his shortcomings or incompetence, and is apparently oblivious to feedback or warnings. He is very hard to deal with, because there is no recognition of his weaknesses. Patience here will, nine times out of ten, go unrewarded. Shift him if possible to a different job where his skills are more appropriate. If no such job exists in your domain, he will have to be exported. Try to avoid Mr Insouciant taking up too much of your time on his way to the airport.

Be outward looking

Of necessity, you will have to spend most of your first ten days inside your unit and talking to your people. On the other hand, it is important to position yourself and your team as looking outside the unit towards the rest of the organisation and the wider world beyond, especially those who are your customers or can benefit from what you do. Therefore you should do two things, even in the busy first two weeks.

First, you should show as much interest as possible in the broader world, asking questions of your people and making it clear that you see the unit's role in an outgoing way.

Second, you should make at least one important excursion to the outside world (to other parts of the organisation or to customers), which will serve as a symbol of your commitment to the outside.

After the first two weeks, you should spend at least a third of your time 'on the outside'.

Communicate by actions

We have already stressed the importance of one or more symbolic actions to demonstrate your values, commitment and cause. You should have worked at least one of these out before you arrive.

Now is the time to follow through with maximum effect. Do not do anything you do not believe in, or which is not characteristic; but early exaggeration or caricature of a true attribute is helpful. For example, if you think the team has become too keen on clock watching, and you normally arrive at 8 a.m. (or leave at 7 p.m.), it would be no bad thing to arrive for the first two weeks at 7 a.m. (or leave at 8 p.m.).

How you spend your time, the questions you ask and the way you interact with other people will all be keenly noted. It is possible to communicate an extraordinary amount via these means, without ever saying anything directly to enunciate your values or Cause.

Create allies

Another part of your preparation, creating allies (see

list on pages 24–26, above), also needs to start being implemented. Carefully pursue the people previously targeted, as well as being on the lookout for potential new allies.

As always in life, the best way to store up future help is to give your desired allies something in the first place. This need not be very lavish: a courtesy here, a piece of corporate support there, a modest but unexpected service to a customer, or simply a sign that you recognise the person's existence and importance.

Remember also the importance of having your own people in your area, and see whether there is any way you can properly justify hiring a newcomer whom you know and trust. Many people feel embarrassed about this or worry that it is somehow slightly illegitimate. These are unhelpful and unfounded vestiges of social reserve. Nothing could be more helpful to the organisation than bringing in excellent people who can further enhance your effectiveness and that of the team as a whole.

Keep close to your boss

Another tricky issue, where reserve often gives the wrong answer, is the extent and nature of early interaction with your boss. Many newly appointed bosses feel that they should steer clear of their boss(es) – the person or people who appointed them – until they know exactly what they are doing and can talk authoritatively about the new position.

Such reserve is understandable, but naïve and unhelpful. It is naïve, because no seasoned superboss expects you to be totally on top of the job in your first week (in fact, the superboss is likely to be repelled by any suggestion that you know everything on day two). And it is unhelpful, to you, the team and the superboss, because of all the people in the organisation, only the superboss really has a vested interest in your success (because he or she picked you). The superboss should really want to help you in the critical early days, and has the corporate clout and the knowledge to do so.

So be open about the challenges and the difficulties you face, and leave it open for the superboss to comment or help (or not). If you read this book, you should be well prepared and, far from thinking worse of you because you are aware of difficulties, the superboss should be impressed by the speed with which you have spotted the pitfalls and by your determination to create a centre of excellence.

Take stock after ten days

The first ten days will have been a busy and demanding time (all the more reason to be fit and relaxed before you start). Take the test below to see how well you have done. Then shut this book, and ensure you have a work-free and enjoyable weekend.

The day ten checklist

1 Have you identified whether you have any box 3 and box 4 people, and who they are?

Tick

A I have no idea what you're talking about ☐

B Not yet/not sure ☐

C Yes ☐

2 Have you worked out what to do with your box 3 people?

A Yes ☐

B No/not yet ☐

3 Have you spent at least one hour in private conversation with each of your direct reports?

A Yes ☐

B No ☐

4 Do you know what your team can and should be doing for your organisation, and for the outside world?

A Yes, roughly at least ☐

B I have some idea and will refine it later ☐

C No, it's too early ☐

5 Have you confirmed your view about the team's competitive position and how it can remain or become better than 'similar' teams?

A Yes ☐

B No ☐

6 Have you been more assertive than usual?

A No, because no great change is necessary and I am normally quite assertive enough, thank you ☐

B No, I recognise the need for change, but I am biding my time until I can prove this fully ☐

C No, because actions speak louder than words and my actions should have demonstrated to anyone with half a brain what I think needs to be done ☐

D Yes, because there need to be changes and people should recognise this from the start ☐

7 Have you spent at least two hours in total in the last two weeks talking to your boss?

A No, I want to wait until I am on top of the job ☐

B No, I wanted to but couldn't get in to see him or her ☐

C Yes ☐

8 Where have you spent most of the last two weeks?

A With my team, getting to know them and the organisation ☐

B In my office, trying to work out how the business works and writing my plan ☐

C Visiting customers ☐

D Elsewhere ☐

9 Have you worked/do you plan to work for some time during each of the first two weekends in the job?

A Yes ☐

B No ☐

SCORING YOUR ANSWERS

Question 1
For A or B, score 0
For C, score 15

Question 2
For A, score 15
For B, score 0

Question 3
For A, score 10
For B, score 0

Question 4
For A or B, score 10
For C, score 0

Question 5
For A, score 10
For B, score 0

Question 6
For A, score 10
For B, score 0
For C or D, score 10

Question 7
For A or B, score 0
For C, score 10

Question 8

For A, score 10
For B, C or D, score 0

Question 9

For A, score 0
For B, score 10

INTERPRETING YOUR SCORES

80–100 points	Well done! You have made an excellent start and can feel a lot more confident now than you did two weeks ago.
60–75 points	Not too bad. Highlight the things you have not yet done and make sure that you plug the gap during the next week or so. I know it's difficult, but grasping nettles now will avoid letting the garden get out of control later.
40–55 points	You are trying but you are not prioritising the right things. Think very carefully about how you can make up for lost time during the next week. Do this by cutting out some things that you were planning to do that are really not essential.
0–35 points	You are either not reading this book carefully enough or else you are not being tough enough in doing the things you know are right. Take a deep breath, cancel your plans for the next two weeks and have another go at doing what this chapter suggests. Your first 100 days may have to last 120, but probably no one will notice. But you must get it right now.

4

Bosses and markets

You should have spent the last two weeks with your team, with some thought and a little time devoted to customers and your boss. The next two weeks should be spent focusing on the outside world, starting with your market, clients and customers.

But I don't have customers or clients!

Wrong! Everyone has customers or clients. OK, they may not be called that, and they may not actually pass money across for purchases, but every unit serves some economic purpose (unless you work as part of an unenlightened, Soviet-style bureaucracy and most of these are now dead or dying). Every unit should benefit some people outside the unit. If you think you don't have clients or customers, work out who these people are and think of them from now on as your clients. Your clients may be inside your firm or stakeholders outside it, but they are there and your future depends on satisfying them.

Study your opinion polls

You may think you don't have these either! Really? No customers and no opinion polls? What is the business world coming to?

In fact, by 'opinion polls' I mean the measures of how well your unit is performing for its customers, in their opinion.

Many businesses selling consumer goods like toothpaste or cars do literally have opinion polls, in the form of Nielsen or AGB data showing market shares and customer satisfaction ratings. But all teams should have the functional equivalent of such data. They should know how much their services are in demand, and how customers think about them, both in their own right and when compared to competing providers of similar products or services.

If you have been appointed switchboard supervisor, your customers are people outside the firm who are trying to call in, as well as people inside the firm wanting to receive such calls and also make their own calls. For you, the relevant data are things like how many times the phone rings before it is answered, how often people are put on hold and how long they spend in the loop before getting to the person they want, how friendly people think the operators are and how all of these points compare to their experience when phoning other organisations.

Whatever business you are in, and whatever your team does in the company, you should be able to think of comparable measures of performance and popularity among your customers. Work out with your team as creatively as possible what the measures of customer satisfaction should be and how to compare them with those of your competitors.

Having worked out the measures, you can then go on to think about how to collect the data. No doubt you will already have some data to go on on some of the points, even if they are only anecdotal or negative (complaints). The trouble is that much of this information, although valid and valuable, is of an exceptional nature, so you will need to take some samples of information at random. Whenever possible, try to get the respondents to score you and 'competitors' on a numerical (say, one to ten or one to five) scale, as well as collecting more qualitative comments.

For instance, a charity helping young people in trouble wanted to know what the people who dealt with it (both the young people and also other bodies providing funds or help of some sort, like probation officers, health officials, magistrates and local authorities) thought about the charity. A simple telephone survey was developed asking the 'customers' to rate the charity out of ten on five characteristics and then the 'customers' were asked to do the same for other charities like Barnados or Save The Children. The results were then compared as follows.

	Charity X	*'Competitors'*
Caring Approach	8.9	7.5
Responsiveness to Customers	8.4	5.7
Innovation	8.3	6.0
Cost effectiveness	6.3	5.5
Internal efficiency	6.1	6.2
Financial resources	4.8	8.3
Fund raising ability	4.4	8.2

Among other things, this small survey highlighted the need for the charity to spend more money and devote more time to fund raising, and gave it the confidence to expand its operations, secure in the knowledge that its customers rated its sharp-end work very highly.

Another approach which is very often helpful is to ask customers which things are most important to them when deciding which product to buy or service to use. Rated again on a one to ten scale, this information can then be used to classify customers into particular 'segments', which each contain people with similar needs, but different from the needs of people in other segments.

A good example of this is a survey of customers buying a particular type of clothing. Research showed that there were three almost equally important needs in the market as a whole:

Clothing Market Purchase Criteria

	Total market
Price	7.6
Quality/durability	7.5
Style/fashion	7.5

This information may look useful, but it is a difficult job to make clothing to satisfy all three needs. Much more useful was the classification of the customers into three different groups or segments, for each of which there was one clearly dominant need.

Clothing Market Segmented Purchase Criteria

	Segment A	*Segment B*	*Segment C*
Price	9.3	6.7	6.8
Quality/durability	7.0	9.5	6.0
Style/fashion	4.9	7.9	9.7

With this information, it is clear that the clothing supplier should not try to satisfy all demands of the market equally, because the supplier would end up satisfying none of the particularly strong needs of any segment or customer. It is far more sensible for each supplier to find out how it is rated in each segment (and on each purchase criterion), and then to concentrate on the segment that plays to its strengths. For example, a low cost supplier might decide to focus on Segment A (the price segment), providing clothes at a very reasonable price and of quite good quality, but not worrying about style or fashion. Another firm might focus on segment B (the quality segment), charging a fair bit more for the product but ensuring excellent durability, and also paying quite a bit of attention to style. A third competitor might target segment C (the fashion segment), not caring if its clothes wore out quickly or were at a premium price, but hiring the best designers, models and advertisers to ensure a chic reputation. This way all three companies could satisfy their own customers, avoid too much direct competition and each make a good profit.

Think about what the customer segments in your business might be and where your team is likely to score highest, either now or with a few relatively easy adjustments. Wherever possible, gather the information to enable you to decide which customers and customer needs to target for excellence, and to monitor how well you are doing as you go along.

Once you have focused on your customers and their needs, this will provide a natural and relatively painless way of reforming your unit and improving your team's performance. It will no longer be you, the big bad boss, standing over your people, hectoring and bullying them to jump higher. Instead, you will be the guide and trainer, pointing out what the team's customers (who will decide whether it prospers) want, and helping the team to organise itself to gain more and happier customers. The ideal situation is when each team member does this automatically, leaving you free to think about the next major strategic move forward for the team.

Practical ways to focus the team on customers

Here are some practical suggestions about how to spend these two weeks to maximum effect.

- Commission one or more team members to pull together all the information the unit possesses on customers already. This should take at most a day or so and then you should get the whole team in a room to get to grips with what the data are saying. This will be useful even (or especially) if you discover that you have little or no such data, making the telling point that procedures and attitudes will have to change. If there is lots of information, it is likely that there are some very valuable lessons that have been forgotten or never properly learnt.
- Get the team to summarise who its most important customers are and what their most important needs are.
- Then ask the team to consider how well it is doing on these needs, both in absolute terms and also relative to competition.
- Introduce the idea of customer segments and ask the team to identify the segment or segments it can best serve, and what is the most important thing to do for each segment.
- Get the team to organise a number (3 to 12) of customer visits for you to attend as the new boss. These could be for customers to come to you or for you to go to them, as they prefer. Ensure that some of your own people are there with you. You can ask relatively detached questions (like, what are we good at and not so good at or what are the most important things for us to do to satisfy you) in your role as the new person around. You and your team will almost certainly learn things that they were not fully aware of before. Ensure that the

results of each meeting, in terms of insight into customer needs, are shared with the team, if possible in informal group meetings. Where possible, attribute praise on particular points to individuals in the team, but couch blame or under-performance in collective terms. The team should enjoy these sessions, or they will be reluctant to learn from them.

- Secure a collective commitment to whatever improvements are necessary, ensure that individual responsibility and accountability for action steps are identified and agreed, and set in place the monitoring which will enable the team and individuals to see how well they are doing.

All of this should be set in motion during these two weeks, so you will need to set aside a lot of time (perhaps even most of the time) to accomplish it. If the demands of your team's work make it impossible to do all this during normal working hours, get their agreement to meet in the evenings or at some other time. If you don't face the challenge of customers early on in the process in a concentrated way, people will assume that it is not a very high priority for you or for them, and time spent in the future on thinking about customers will pay much poorer dividends. So do whatever is necessary to give it full attention now.

Customers should be the main agenda item for you in these two weeks, but you should also spend a fair amount of time thinking about and meeting your boss or bosses.

How to deal with bosses

The first mental step is to realise that your boss is there to help. Yes, seriously! Just as your job is to make your direct

reports more effective, so too one of your boss's roles, for which he or she is paid, is to make you a success. Too often, as a hangover from the bad old days of scientific management and the dark satanic mills, we retain in our minds a vestige of the boss as ogre. Consequently we grovel, we act deferentially, we sweat in his or her presence, we think we have to be on our best behaviour or we simply try to stay out of the way.

None of this is rational behaviour. It is in no one's interests: not yours, not your team's, and certainly not your boss's (unless he or she is power crazed, in which case you have a much bigger problem than can be addressed here).

So in this case we have to invert Kennedy's dictum: ask not what you can do for the boss (not yet anyway), but what the boss can do for you.

The chances are, in the early days, the boss can do a great deal for you. Consider this under at least the following headings.

INFORMATION

Almost certainly, your boss will know a great deal more about the lie of the internal political land than you do. The boss will probably also know a lot about the needs and quirks of important customers and other stakeholders. Make sure that you tap into this data base as quickly and fully as possible.

UPWARD SUPPORT

You will quickly realise the need for some extra resources if you are to push your team forward to achieve excellent results. You may need more people, more money or the full co-operation of another part of your organisation. Only your boss can obtain these things for you. Your first job, then, is to explain to and persuade the boss that these things are needed for the benefit of the firm as a whole. A practical hint here is that when asking for more of something, you should at the same time offer to use less of a less essential resource. So, where possible, also offer to give up a person (perhaps one of your box 3s!), part of the budget or inessential services from another unit. This will make it clear that you are thinking corporately and are not on an empire-building kick.

DOWNWARD SUPPORT

Unless you are a saint and a fixer rolled into one (St Paul would qualify, most other saints or fixers would not), you will experience some difficulties getting your team to do what is necessary. There will almost certainly be some recalcitrance and back sliding from some individuals in the team, and they may have quite a 'bank account' of goodwill elsewhere in the firm, possibly at some high levels. You will therefore need the implicit political backing of your boss or bosses in pushing through your reforms (even if these are supported by most of your team). Make sure, therefore, that your boss is fully aware of any potential difficulties, and fully briefed about why contentious issues may arise and why it is necessary to confront them, so that your boss may be a persuasive advocate of your cause if any problems come to the attention of senior management. In some cases the boss may also be of direct assistance in helping to pull any difficult team members into line (but let the boss volunteer such help; never ask for it directly).

COMRADESHIP AND MORAL SUPPORT

Do not underestimate the potential emotional strain of taking on a new job and attempting to do it better. 'If it isn't hurting, it isn't working.' You will need some support, a sounding board and a sympathetic ear from time to time. Key allies in your team and elsewhere in the firm at your level can supply some of this need, but help from a boss has a particularly refreshing value here. Here again, however, be sensitive. Do not ask for what is not going to be given. Put yourself in a position where such help can be forthcoming, rather than being importunate in demanding it.

Bosses are idiosyncratic and have 'hot buttons'

Bosses are all human beings, but they are all different. (This is a trite, universal truth, but I do not apologise for pointing it out, because it is important. Read on to see why.) Just as it is important for you to discover what really excites customers, so it is valuable to discover what really gets the attention and support of your boss. In American slang these excitement and approval generators are called 'hot buttons'. You need to know what your boss's hot buttons are.

For example, some bosses are turned on by numbers. They are analysts. They love playing with their calculators. They think they are rationalists. They care not for emotions or causes, they disdain opinions and instincts, and their favourite expression is 'bring me the facts'. If your boss is one of these, you would not get off to a great start by talking about your Cause, your vision or your gut feelings. You would be better advised to work out a careful cost benefit analysis for any step you propose.

But other bosses are charismatic leaders for whom numbers are backup to be relegated to the accountants and the rocket scientists, and for whom the real issues relate to driving the business forward, and inspiring flesh and blood people: customers, employees, competitors. These bosses may be careless about detail but good at the 'vision thing'. A cost benefit analysis would leave such a person cold.

Other bosses have little time for numbers or philosophy, but are intensely practical and pragmatic. They want to think about actions, the thick of the battle and practical results. They are fascinated by the politics of business and enjoy nothing so much as a good arm twisting. They are good people to discuss recalcitrant team members with, but not so responsive to discussions of your cause or your cost benefit analysis.

These stereotypes of bosses are discussed further in the next chapter, in relation to your own characteristics. Of course, they are only one way of describing people, containing no more than fragments of the truth. If you can find additional or different ways of describing your boss's personal characteristics and 'world view', do so as fully as you can. Before you see your boss, and while you are with him or her, try to identify what their hot buttons are, and to the extent that you honestly can, play on these hot buttons to establish empathy and common purpose, and to get practical support for your efforts.

In getting your boss's support, try to look at the approaches that others use and at their relative success or failure. Wherever possible, look back at corporate history and see what has made your boss successful and influential, and what his or her natural strengths are. This will help you to understand when and how to get support for your own programme.

Do not neglect the 'superbosses'

A superboss is your boss's boss or bosses. Assess whenever you can who among these is likely to be an ally for your cause, what the relationship of your boss to the superboss is, and what are the hot buttons of the superboss. Gradually develop and refine this knowledge, but use it economically and with sensitivity. Do not 'go over your boss's head'. But try, wherever possible, to give exposure and visibility to anything you are doing that is clearly in the interests of the company as a whole, and likely to secure and benefit from the support of appropriate superbosses.

On to the day 20 checklist

You should now be ready to review your progress over the last two weeks and the checklist below awaits you. No doubt you have had an interesting fortnight: we shall see in a moment how successful it has been.

The day 20 checklist

1 Have you identified your customers and obtained all available information about their key needs and what they think of your unit?

Tick

A Yes, but there isn't much information available ☐

B Yes, and the information is very helpful ☐

C No, not yet, we're still working on it to get a fuller picture ☐

D No, it's too early to worry about all this ☐

2 Have you identified your opinion polls? ☐

A Yes ☐

B They don't yet exist, but we are well on the way to creating them ☐

No ☐

3 Can you define at least three customer segments of relevance to your unit?

A No ☐

B Yes ☐

C Not yet, but we are working hard on this and will have it soon ☐

4 Do you know which one or two segments have the best fit with your team and its capabilities?

A Yes, we've already got a pretty good idea ☐

B We have some hypotheses and are testing them out ☐

C To be honest, we don't have much idea at all yet ☐

5 Have you had at least one general meeting of your team to talk about customer needs and segments?

A Yes ☐

B No ☐

6 Have you already had at least three meetings with key customers?

A Yes ☐

B Not yet ☐

7 Have you fed back results of these customers' meetings and discussed them with your team?

A Yes ☐

B No/not applicable (because the meetings haven't happened yet) ☐

8 Has your team agreed an action plan to improve customer satisfaction with identified individual responsibilities and deadlines?

A Yes ☐

B No ☐

9 Have you already mobilised the support of your boss in the potential areas where he or she could help you (information; upward support; downward support; comradeship)?

A No ☐

B In one area only ☐

C In two areas ☐

D Yes, in three or four areas ☐

10 Could you describe in a few words your boss's main hot buttons?

A I beg your pardon! ☐

B I'm working on it ☐

C Yes ☐

SCORING YOUR ANSWERS

Question 1

For A or B, score 10 points
For C, score 5 points
For D, score 0

Question 2

For A, score 15 points
For B, score 5 points
For C, score 0

Question 3

For A, score 0
For B, score 10 points
For C, score 0

Question 4

For A, score 15 points
For B, score 5 points
For C, score 0

Questions 5 to 8

For **each** A, score 10 points
For **each** B, score 0

Question 9

For A, score 0
For B, score 10

For C, score 15
For D, score 20

Question 10
For A or B, score 0
For C, score 10

INTERPRETING YOUR SCORES

100–120 points Congratulations! You are well on top of the issues. See if you can do as well in the next ten days.

80–95 points A reasonable start. Fill in the gaps during the next fortnight.

60–75 points You have made some progress but not enough to go straight on. Spend another week mastering the points you failed on.

0–55 points Oh dear! I am sorry to sound headmasterly, but you really will not be successful unless you apply the principles discussed here. Spend another two weeks on this, or however long is necessary to give you a score of at least 80.

5

Know thyself

If you are like most people, you will enjoy this chapter best. But it is not enough to read it: you do need to discover what sort of person you are and then set certain wheels in motion to ensure that the team has balanced leadership. I am not implying that you are unbalanced, only that you are not perfect!

From the many tests of personality, three are particularly relevant to the new leader:

- the technical skills test
- the introvert/extrovert test
- the Hal Leavitt [1–2–3] test.

The third one is the most fun and most likely to lead you to new insights about yourself, but the first two tests are essential and must be undertaken first.

The technical skills test

This one is easy and quick. Below is a table with three columns. The first column lists certain skills, which may or may not be important for your job. The last three lines have been left blank for you to write in any particularly relevant skills which are not listed already. For each category of skill, first score how far your job requires each skill on a 1–10 scale, where 1 is totally unnecessary and 10 is essential. Then (and only then) go down the second column and assess honestly how far you personally have these skills today, on a similar 1–10 scale, where 1 means you have no such skills and 10 that you are an expert. Finally, subtract column 2 from column 1 to arrive at the third column, the Skill Gap measure. A positive number in the third column means there is a Skill Gap. A zero or a negative number indicates that there is no skill gap (a negative number means that you have more than enough skill, although this should not be a problem!).

You should now circle any skill where both of the following conditions apply: the first column number is 5 or more and the last column number is 2 or more; that is, where the skill is reasonably important for the job and where you have a definite skill gap. Clearly, for skills circled, the higher the number in either the first or the third column, the more serious the matter is.

Do not be alarmed if you find you have a skill gap or even several. Many very successful bosses have coped with large and important Skill Gaps. The way to do this is not to pretend to have skills you don't (someone will always find you out), but to depend on one of your direct reports honestly and openly for a skill in which you are deficient but in which he or she is an expert.

Of course, you have to ensure that the person really does have the skill, and you also have to ensure that it is being sensibly deployed and that you are still thinking about the overall policy issues, so that you ask the technical expert the right questions and do not automatically follow his or her advice. But the 'plain person' approach, where you ask the right questions and use your common sense, while leaving the technicians to work their magic, can be much more effective than getting by on your own on a sketchy

Skill	1 Job needs	2 My skills	3 Skill gap
Financial and accounting			
Numeracy			
Engineering			
Report writing			
Interpersonal			
Analytical			
Industry knowledge			
Interaction with government			
Dealing with trade unions			
Negotiation			
Public relations			
Dealing with customers			
Public speaking			
Dealing with banks and/or the City			
Computing/systems			
Creativity/imagination			
Attention to detail			
Caution/conservatism			

skill base. It can also bind you positively to the direct reports concerned and make their job much more fulfilling.

You do have a problem, however, if your Skill Gap(s) cannot be covered by one of your direct reports. If this is the case, you must either promote someone from further down to be one of your direct reports, provided he or she does have the skill and is of the right general calibre to be promoted, or hire in someone, from another part of the company or from outside, with extreme dispatch. Do not delay; start the process today. All too often new bosses either kid themselves that a Skill Gap does not exist or that it is unimportant, or else think it is something that can be addressed later. There are often good reasons for being dilatory: it may be difficult to get approval for a new hire, bringing in someone from outside may upset the pecking order among your current team and so on. But however good the reason may appear, it is a trap. A serious Skill Gap could set the team off in the wrong direction and seriously endanger your personal credibility in the organisation. It is a risk that must not be taken.

Do not be afraid to change the organisation and job roles to fit your Skill Gap and personal inclination needs, whether or not you need to import another person into your team. For example, the chief executive who has flair and charisma, and is good at selling, may not be good at paying attention to detail and administration. The organisation may at the moment have a number of functional heads (finance, engineering, research, marketing etc.) reporting directly to the chief executive. If he or she is wise, they will create a new post of chief operating officer between them and the rest of the team, although continuing to have lots of personal contact with the functional heads. (It never ceases to amaze me how little this simple and effective tactic is used. People tend to accept the organisational status as holy and immutable, especially early in their jobs. This is the best possible time to change it, before people settle into ineffective routines.)

Look again at the areas where you are strongest (that have the highest scores in the second column of the table above). If the job does not currently focus very much on these areas (i.e. there is a lower number in the first column and therefore a negative number in the third column), think for a while about the possibility of changing the job over time so that it plays more to your strengths.

This may be impossible and dangerous – for example, you may be very good at taking risks, but if you are an airline pilot for British Airways who happens to be good at flying upside down it would not be sensible to expose passengers to unnecessary risks just because you usually get away with them. But it may be possible and appropriate. You might now be a marketing director who has also had experience of being head of production. Using your production knowledge, you might want to focus your sales and marketing efforts more on the type of customers for whom goods can be made more easily and cheaply. You could naturally develop a very close and fruitful relationship between marketing and production, which perhaps did not exist at all before you were appointed marketing director.

Now is probably the time to take a break and reflect on what you have learned about your skills and to decide on any action plan necessary (or better still, to start to take the action now). Come back in a while for the next two personality tests.

The introvert/extrovert test

A surprising number of people believe they are extroverts when in fact they are not. So, whatever you think you are, go quickly down the list of questions below and tick (a) or (b) for each question. If you don't much like either answer, select the one for which you have a marginal preference (do not leave any question unanswered).

1 Do you prefer:

Tick

(a) for people to know who you are when you are in public, or ☐

(b) to be anonymous. ☐

2 Do you like walking alone sometimes?

(a) No ☐

(b) Yes ☐

3 When you are writing something, do you like to be interrupted by a friend on the phone?

(a) Yes ☐

(b) No ☐

4 Do you get lonely if you see no one all day?

(a) No ☐

(b) Yes ☐

5 Do you prefer evenings to mornings?

(a) Yes ☐

(b) No ☐

6 Are you the life and soul of the party?

(a) Not usually ☐

(b) Nearly always ☐

7 Do you usually think carefully before you speak?

(a) No ☐

(b) Yes ☐

8 Do you like meeting new people at parties, or prefer just to see old friends whom you know you will enjoy seeing?

(a) New people ☐

(b) Old friends ☐

9 Do you have friends round for a meal at least once a fortnight?

(a) Yes ☐

(b) No ☐

10 Do you prefer the countryside or the town?

(a) Countryside ☐

(b) Town ☐

11 Do you have more than ten people you would consider close friends?

(a) Yes ☐

(b) No ☐

12 Do you sometimes sing or whistle in the street?
(a) No ☐
(b) Yes ☐

13 Are you vain?
(a) Yes ☐
(b) No ☐

14 If you went to the races, would you back favourites or outsiders?
(a) Outsiders ☐
(b) Favourites ☐

15 Do you like riding round in an open-top sports car?
(a) Yes ☐
(b) No ☐

16 Are you usually in a rush?
(a) Yes ☐
(b) No ☐

17 Do you usually turn up on time for appointments?
(a) Sometimes late ☐
(b) Usually on time ☐

18 Are you generally tidy, both at work and at home?
(a) Yes ☐
(b) No ☐

19 When catching a train or a plane, do you usually allow plenty of extra time in case something delays you on the way?

(a) No ☐

(b) Yes ☐

20 Do you often wear colourful clothes?

(a) Not often ☐

(b) Yes ☐

21 Can you usually wake up without an alarm clock?

(a) No ☐

(b) Yes ☐

22 Do you usually drive faster than most people?

(a) No ☐

(b) Yes ☐

23 Do you enjoy a quiet read (or listening to music) in bed?

(a) Rarely ☐

(b) Yes, quite often ☐

24 Think of your spouse or closest partner. Are they more outgoing than you?

(a) Yes ☐

(b) No ☐

25 Are you a thoughtful, reflective person or do you prefer action?

(a) Action ☐

(b) Thoughtful ☐

26 When in a foreign country whose language you know poorly, do you hesitate before approaching someone to ask for directions?

(a) Yes ☐

(b) No ☐

27 Do you sometimes swear?

(a) Yes ☐

(b) Almost never ☐

28 Do you like dancing?

(a) Not much ☐

(b) Yes ☐

29 In a group, do you often volunteer your services?

(a) Yes ☐

(b) No ☐

30 If you were in conversation with three other people, on a subject you all knew well, would you speak more than a quarter of the time?

(a) No ☐

(b) Yes ☐

31 Do you quite often talk to strangers, when there is no need to do so?

(a) Yes ☐

(b) No ☐

32 Do you sometimes poke your nose into other people's business?

(a) Yes, quite often ☐

(b) Almost never ☐

33 Do you like eating out on your own sometimes?

(a) Yes ☐

(b) Not much ☐

SCORING YOUR ANSWERS

For questions 4, 6, 10, 12, 18, 20, 22, 24, 26, 28 and 30, score minus 3 for each (a) answer and plus 3 for each (b) answer. On all other questions, score plus 3 for each (a) answer and minus 3 for each (b) answer.

Theoretically, you could score between minus 99 and plus 99. In practice, most people score between minus 39 and plus 39. A positive score indicates extroversion and a negative score introversion.

plus 42 to plus 99	You really are unusually extrovert and should pay particular attention to the remarks below for extroverts.

plus 18 to plus 39	You are a 'normal' extrovert. See below.
minus 15 to plus 15	You have a balance of introvert and extrovert characteristics. You therefore do not need to take any of the 'corrective' measures we suggest below for extroverts and introverts.
minus 18 to minus 39	You are a 'normal' introvert, with some extrovert tendencies but a preponderance of introversion. See comments for introverts below.
minus 42 to minus 99	You are unusually introverted. This is nothing to worry about, as some great leaders were also very introverted (Clement Atlee and Sir Owen Green for example, founders, respectively, of the UK welfare state and one of Britain's most successful conglomerates, BTR). But see below for advice on how to make sure your introversion is not a liability.

ADVICE FOR EXTROVERT BOSSES

You certainly need advice, as you tend towards being a little cocky. The higher your positive score on the test, the more you should pay attention to the hints below.

- **Do not take important decisions 'off the cuff'.** Make sure that you obtain advice and guidance from qualified colleagues before committing yourself. Do not trust excessively in your own judgement.
- **Pay attention to detail.** This is probably not one of your strong suits, but try to stop being cavalier with

facts or delegating every detail matter to a team member. On the really important issues, take pride in being a master of the facts in detail.

- **Do not assume that because someone isn't talking, or is slow to react, that they are not thinking or feeling very much.** Do not project your own ways of behaving on to others. Try to be sensitive to their thought processes, look for the non-verbal signs, and be more patient and diplomatic than comes naturally, particularly with customers. Try to become a good listener, which is much more difficult than being a good talker.

- **Do not take unnecessary risks.** Extroverts usually enjoy taking risks and often make very good entrepreneurs. But if your job doesn't really require this, and especially if wrong decisions could end in disaster, try to curb your natural inclinations and wait until you are away from work to gratify your risk-taking needs.

- **Try not to dominate your team members.** Too many extrovert bosses do not delegate effectively. They may say and think that they want to delegate, but, without intending to, they inhibit people really picking up the ball and running with it. So, when someone takes a decision which is in their sphere of authority, when you would have made the opposite call, do not point this out, especially if the decision proves to be wrong in practice. Also, if someone refers a decision to you, resist the temptation to make the decision wherever possible, and make the individual really take his or her own decision. A good idea is to stay away from the office from time to time, make only absolutely essential phone calls in and force people to make their own decisions that way.

When on holiday, do not leave your phone number and do not call into the office.

ADVICE FOR INTROVERT BOSSES

- **Select an extrovert 'running mate'.** A 'running mate' is the American vice-presidential candidate paired up with the presidential candidate, and is usually selected to provide an ideological and geographical contrast to the main candidate, so as to arrive at a 'balanced ticket'. The same concept is useful here. As boss, you have to ensure that what you want is communicated to your people, and that information flows freely around your unit. Even more importantly, you need to communicate to the outside world. Now, communication by action is the best method and introverts are just as good at this as extroverts (and often better). You can also communicate by the written word. But even though it is not as efficient, most people like to experience communication through the spoken word instead of or in addition to the other methods. This is not your natural style. To some extent you can force yourself to communicate, but this will never be a total solution. What you therefore need to do is find a 'running mate' with whom you feel comfortable and maintain very close contact, so that the 'running mate' can then act as a major conduit of information for you, both from you to others and from others to you. The 'running mate' can be a deputy to you, but need not be that senior, as long as he or she has your confidence and the respect of the rest of your team. A personal assistant or secretary can very often fulfil this role amazingly well. But make sure that the 'running mate' really does have a sufficient dose of extroversion to offset your introversion.
- **Do not cut yourself off from the team.** Introverts do

not have the same (inefficient) social needs at work as extroverts. You will therefore rarely be seen lounging around near the coffee machine or suggesting a drink after work to some of your team. You may want the peace and quiet of your own office, with the door firmly shut and the telephone rigorously screened by your secretary. But beware. These perfectly reasonable characteristics can easily be misinterpreted as a lack of care for your team or indifference to their feelings. So make a point of being as accessible as you can, encourage your secretary to make it easy for people to see you, and hold regular communication meetings at a fixed time when you solicit feedback and questions.

- **See the big picture.** Most introverts are very good at detail, but many are not so good at 'the vision thing', the overall direction and purpose for the unit or firm. Especially if you don't feel a natural empathy with these rather nebulous concepts, pay a great deal of attention to them, because they are important. Do not skip the sections of this book (e.g. pages 38–40) which deal with 'mission' and 'vision'.
- **Take occasional risks.** Most introverts are risk averse and therefore avoid making bad mistakes. Sometimes, however, there is a lot to be gained by taking a calculated risk. Do not always be excessively cautious: go against your natural inclination on occasion. And even if the gamble fails, do not decide never to take a risk again!

The Hal Leavitt [1–2–3] Test

Now for the third and, in many ways, the most interesting test of all. Harold ('Hal') Leavitt, that great

American sage of human behaviour, taught me this test,* but no doubt I have perverted his doctrine somewhat, so I apologise to him if this is a garbled version. The insight, I hasten to add, is his, not mine. (The specific test questions below were, however, developed by me without reference to him.)

THREE TYPES OF PEOPLE

Leavitt categorises leaders into three types. All can be extremely effective (or destructive), but each type leads by quite different means.

- **Type 1: The Visionary** This is perhaps the type of leader most people would expect: bold, charismatic, original, often eccentric, brilliant and uncompromising, someone who offers a clear break with the present and a dream of what could be in the future. Raiding history's storehouse for examples, type 1s would include Jesus Christ, Gladstone, Garibaldi, Ghandi, Churchill, Hitler, John F. Kennedy, Martin Luther King, Margaret Thatcher and the Ayatollah Khomeni. All of these had insights and dreams which were revolutionary; all provided inspiration to their followers; and all were at times extremely impractical and bad at getting things done. After all, what could be less practical than Martin Luther King's tingling declaration, 'I have a dream'?
- **Type 2: The Analyst** This is the leader who is also brilliant, but who deals with numbers and facts rather than dreams and opinions. The analyst is a rationalist who believes that 'If something cannot be reduced to numbers, it is meaningless'. The analyst tends to deal in black and white rather than shades of grey: there is a right answer somewhere, as long as the necessary facts

* Leavitt, Hal, 1–2–3 test (*Corporate Pathfinders*, Penguin Books, London, 1986) 69, 83–91.

can be collected and analysed. The analyst can use numbers and accounting conventions to control a vast empire in a regular, predictable and understandable way. Business tends to be stocked more with analysts than the corridors of history: examples include the two introverts cited earlier, Clement Atlee and Sir Owen Green, as well as Robert Macnamara, Arnold Weinstock and Harold Geneen. Political parallels would also take in Pitt the Younger, Sir Robert Peel, Harold Wilson and Jimmy Carter.

- **Type 3: The Doer** This is the genius of action: the implementer, fixer and successful pragmatist. Generally unencumbered by vision or analysis, the type 3 leader loves to twist arms, marshal forces and get things done. Examples from history include Noah, Attila the Hun, Alexander the Great, Julius Caesar, Louis XIV, Napoleon, Bismarck, Lloyd George, Lenin, Stalin, Eisenhower, James Callaghan and Lyndon Johnson.

Most people are not 'pure' types, in that they have classic type 1, 2 or 3 characteristics and none of the others, but all leaders have a dominant streak in one of these three directions that makes them relatively easy to classify. This is also one of those cases where most people are correct in their own self-assessment, so you have probably know already to which group you belong. If you are fed up with tests, you may skip the one below as long as you have a firm idea which type you are and that you support this by asking some friends or colleagues. For the test lover, however, we can make the type diagnosis below.

1 Do you prefer thought to action? *Tick*

(a) Yes ☐

(b) No ☐

2 Do you like saying, 'Bring me facts, not opinions'?

(a) Yes ☐

(b) No ☐

3 Do you believe there is a right and a wrong answer to most questions?

(a) Yes ☐

(b) No ☐

4 Do you believe in God?

(a) Yes ☐

(b) No ☐

5 Do you believe in fate?

(a) Yes ☐

(b) No ☐

6 Have you ever been called 'a bull in a china shop' or something similar?

(a) Yes ☐

(b) No ☐

7 Do you like using a calculator, and do you use one often?

(a) Yes ☐

(b) No ☐

8 Do you like poetry?

(a) Yes ☐

(b) Not much ☐

9 Do you like opera?

(a) Yes ☐

(b) Not much ☐

10 Are you more an extrovert or an introvert?

(a) Extrovert ☐

(b) Introvert ☐

11 Do you like thinking about philosophy?

(a) Yes ☐

(b) Not much ☐

12 Do most people say you are very creative?

(a) Yes ☐

(b) No ☐

13 Are you *particularly* good at getting things done?

(a) Yes ☐

(b) No ☐

14 Are you aggressive?

(a) Yes ☐

(b) No ☐

15 Do you tend to avoid confrontation and argument?

(a) Yes ☐

(b) Not always ☐

16 Could you imagine yourself as a politician?

(a) Sometimes ☐

(b) No ☐

17 Do you prefer dealing with words or numbers?

(a) Words ☐

(b) Numbers ☐

18 Could you imagine yourself as an accountant?

(a) Yes ☐

(b) No ☐

19 Do you quite often let your heart rule your head?

(a) Yes ☐

(b) No ☐

20 Which of these characters are you most like?

(a) Hitler ☐

(b) the Daleks ☐

(c) Attila the Hun ☐

SCORING THE 1–2–3 TEST

The way you score the test is unusual. Each question may or may not generate points for you and there are three different sorts of points which must be scored separately: **black** points, **blue** points and **red** points. Follow the instructions and use the space below to tally up each of the points as you go through your answers.

First tally the black points:

Score 10 black points for **each** of the following answers: if you answered (a) to question 4; (a) to question 5; (a) to question 8; (a) to question 9; (a) to question 11.

Score 20 black points if you answered (a) to question 12.

Score 30 black points if you answered (a) to Question 20.

Now add up the total of black points, which could be between 0 (if you did not give these answers to the questions) and 100.

Next, tally the blue points:

Score 10 blue points for each of the following answers: if you answered (a) to question 2; (a) to question 3; (a) to question 7; (b) to question 10; (b) to Question 17; (a) to question 18; and (b) to question 19.

Score 30 blue points if you answered (b) to question 20.

Now add up the total number of blue points, which again will be between 0 and a hundred.

Finally, tally your number of red points:

Score 10 red points for each of the following answers: if you said (b) to question 1; (a) to question 6; (a) to question 14; (b) to question 15; (a) to question 16.

Score 20 red points if you responded (a) to question 13.

Score 30 red points if you answered (c) to question 20.

Again, add up your total of red points. This will also be between 0 and 100.

YOUR 1–2–3 PROFILE AND WHAT IT MEANS

Now, your 1–2–3 profile can be read as follows: the black points represent your type 1 score, the blue points your type 2 score and the red points your type 3 score. Put them together in this order for your 1–2–3 score.

The highest score represents your dominant trait and the second highest your secondary trait. For example, a score of 20–60–0 would indicate someone whose main characteristics were type 2, with a dash of type 1. Such a person would be very productive in an analytical job which requires a measure of creativity, but which carries no executive responsibilities. A score of 20–10–70 would indicate someone who is a hands-on implementer with common sense and a degree of vision, but almost no inclination for theory and numbers. A score of 50–30–0 could belong to someone with a strong sense of vision, and a creative view of how to build for the future, with some analytical inclination, but hopeless at managing people. A score of 90–10–50 would mean someone unusually strong on creative vision, with little interest in analysis, but with quite a strong interest in practical implementation. Remember that the absolute scores mean little: it is the relative size of the 1–2–3 quotients that matters. Remember also that we are measuring a person's affinities, interests and inclinations, not his or her abilities. There will normally be a correlation with a person's relative abilities under the three headings (for the simple reason that it is easier to be good at something you are interested in) but the test cannot measure one person's actual abilities compared to those of someone else.

ACTION IMPLICATIONS OF YOUR 1–2–3 SCORE

There are two key lessons to be drawn after you have

established your 1–2–3 profile.

- **Move your job more in the direction where your particular skills can be deployed more fully.** For example, if you are a type 1, ensure that a longer term review of strategy and mission is undertaken, and get actively involved. If you are a type 2, make sure that your unit is performing all the problem-solving analyses that could be helpful to the organisation. If you are a type 3, move your unit's mode of operation more towards action.
- **Wherever possible, team up with and rely upon two colleagues who each exemplify the other two types, so that you can act as a fully balanced 1–2–3 team.** You may want to do this with two of your direct reports, with two peers in other organisational units, or even to team up with two of your bosses or other more senior people in the company where you could make an effective team. Balanced 1–2–3 teams can be enormously successful, so try to get into one or more of these wherever possible.

You should now be ready for the day 30 checklist.

The day 30 checklist

1 Have you identified your Skill Gaps?

		Tick
A	Yes	☐
B	Not yet	☐
C	I have taken the test but don't have any Skill Gaps	☐

2 Have you set the wheels in motion to recruit internally or externally so that you have a direct report who will be able to cover each of your Skill Gaps?

A Yes ☐

B Not yet ☐

C Not necessary as I already have direct reports who can do this ☐

3 Have you taken the introvert/extrovert test and scored the answers?

A Yes ☐

B No ☐

4 If you are an extrovert, have you already worked out ways to avoid dominating your team, and started to put these ideas into practice?

A Yes ☐

B Not necessary: I am not an extrovert ☐

C No ☐

5 If you are an introvert, have you selected an extrovert 'running mate' and started to use him or her effectively?

A Yes ☐

B Not necessary: I am not an introvert ☐

C No ☐

6 Have you identified your score on the 1–2–3 test?

A Yes ☐

B No ☐

7 Have you attempted to classify key colleagues on the 1–2–3 test?

A Yes ☐

B No ☐

8 Have you worked out ways to move your job more in the direction of your type strength?

A Yes ☐

B Still thinking about it ☐

C No ☐

9 Have you identified at least one potential 1–2–3 team where you could supply one of the type ingredients and benefit from the other two team members supplying the other two types?

A Yes ☐

B Still thinking about it ☐

C No ☐

SCORING YOUR ANSWERS

Questions 1
For A, score 10 points
For B or C, score 0

Question 2
For A, score 10 points
For B, score 0
For C, score 10 points

Question 3
For A, score 10 points
For B, score 0

Questions 4 and 5

For **each** A or B, score 10 points
For **each** C, score 0

Questions 6 and 7
For **each** A, score 10 points
For **each** B, score 0

Questions 8 and 9
For **each** A, score 15 points
For **each** B , score 5 points
For **each** C, score 0

INTERPRETING YOUR SCORES

80–100 points Another fine performance! If you have really 'known yourself', keep thinking about the implications for your life: new ways of capitalising on this knowledge will constantly arise. Above all, try to get into as many 1–2–3 threesomes as possible!

60–80 points Pick up on those questions where you 'lost' points and try to fill in the gaps. The potential benefit is enormous.

0–55 points You either didn't like the tests or were in too much of a hurry. Reread this chapter when you are more in the mood, and do not move on until you score at least 80.

6

Creating the team

You will recall that the first thing you were advised to do in your first ten days was to get to know your team members. You also assessed them on the attitude/competence matrix (page 36) and were invited to take immediate action on anyone who fell into box 3 of the matrix, that is, who had high competence but a negative attitude. Whatever action you took or did not take then, you should now reassess the team and make sure that you have not ducked any personnel issues. Since then, you will have had a chance to confirm or modify any of your first impressions and should also have gained a better insight into what sort of boss you are, and where you need the team's help to complement your own skills and style. Now is therefore the time to pull all this together and make sure that you take any necessary further action. This should be your main 'off-line' task over the next two weeks.

Person by person

Make a list of all the people who now report to you. Add to this any people further down your own unit whom you think may have the ability or potential to be included in your core team, either now or in the next two years. Finally, add to the list anyone of similar ability or potential elsewhere in the organisation whom you would like to consider as candidates for inclusion in your core team.

Take a page for each person. Reflect and record for him or her the following data.

1 Their position on the attitude/competence matrix (page 36)
2 A list of their top five functional skills (as listed on page 71)
3 Your best guess at where they are on the introvert/extrovert scale (see pages 73–80)
4 Your best guess at their 1–2–3 Profile (see pages 84–91)
5 A list of the three most important things that the individual needs to do to improve his or her performance and potential
6 A definition of the individual's role within the team
7 A list of the three most important ways in which the individual can help you personally in your own job.

Now for some hints on how to go about compiling notes on each individual.

1 THE ATTITUDE/COMPETENCE MATRIX

You may have revised your view of, or effected a change in, each person's position on this matrix. It is reproduced below so that you can put a small circle on it representing each person's position (preferably, fill this in without reference to your earlier positions, though you may be interested afterwards in how your perception and/or their position has changed).

By this stage you should be well advanced in disposing of anyone who still falls in box 3 of the matrix. If you have not done this yet, you must either (preferably) be confident about improving the person's attitude (and hence moving

Revised attitude/competence quadrants

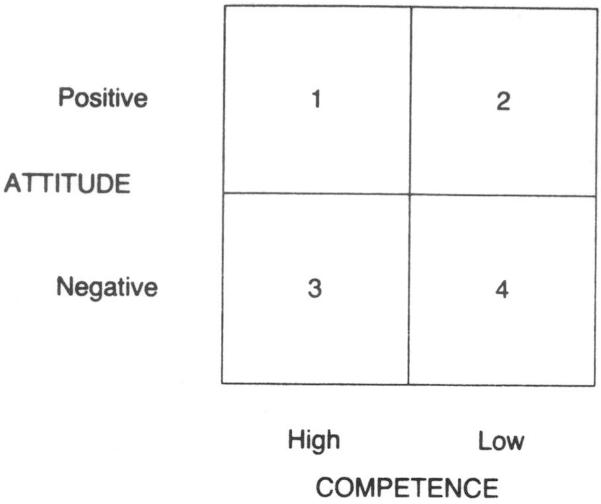

ATTITUDE	High	Low
Positive	1	2
Negative	3	4

COMPETENCE

them to box 1) or else remove the person from your team. This is the last time we shall mention this necessity and is your last opportunity to get rid of any box 3 person before he or she (or they) fatally undermines you. If you do not do this, you are too weak to exert proper leadership and success will probably elude you. Act now or for ever suffer the consequences.

Then there may be some people in box 4 still needing help or relocation. Ideally, a box 4 person should be helped north into box 2, *en route* for box 1 eventually. The other route of going to box 1 via box 3 should be avoided (since box 3 is really a trapdoor out of the matrix and the team!). Deal with the attitude problem before the competence problem. If the attitude cannot be reversed quickly, you need the same resolution as described above to 'export' the individual from your team.

For box 2 people, who deserve and need your help, work

out what needs to be done to move them to box 1. Compile a skill improvement programme (SIP) tailored to their needs as below, taking care to work out who is to be the individual's tutor and assessor in each area.

Skill Improvement Programme for [insert name]

Skill area	Improvement necessary	Tutor	Target date

Ensure that you start the programme going, having briefed each individual and their tutors, before the two weeks are up. Ask for a report from the individual and the tutors from each person on a monthly basis (more frequently if appropriate) and set a target deadline for the completion of the SIP. Generally, six months should be the maximum time allowed. If the person has not successfully completed the SIP and moved to box 1 by then, you will have to resort to the 'export' option. Remember to note and praise any progress along the way, where the person has moved to a satisfactory level of skill on any of the improvement areas.

2 THE PERSON'S TOP FIVE SKILLS

Everyone has their strong suits. For the person you are considering, list in rank order their five most important and outstanding skills (relevant to the tasks your whole team has to accomplish, not just to the job the individual currently does). A useful checklist of possibly relevant skills is given on page 71, but add to this list or create your own if you want.

Then consider how far the person's current job plays to these skills. Can the job description be modified to play more to the skills? If not, and there is still a big gap between the person's potential and their job, consider whether another job in your unit might not be more appropriate, either by a straight swap or by redefining more than one job. You may not reach firm conclusions at this stage, since you are currently considering only one person. When you have been through the seven stages for each person, you may want to revisit this second issue and consider everyone simultaneously, to see whether you need to redefine the team's responsibilities.

3 INTROVERT/EXTROVERT

Recognising that it is a subjective judgement, classify everyone along a continuum of extroversion/introversion. You might want to guess the position of each individual on the scoring scheme described above (pages 73–80), relative to your own position.

The relevance of knowing this is twofold: (1) to ensure that they are yoked up with other team members who can balance any high degree of extroversion or introversion; and (2) so that you can be aware of any counselling needs for highly extrovert or introvert people. The advice you give should be similar to that given to you on pages 82–3!

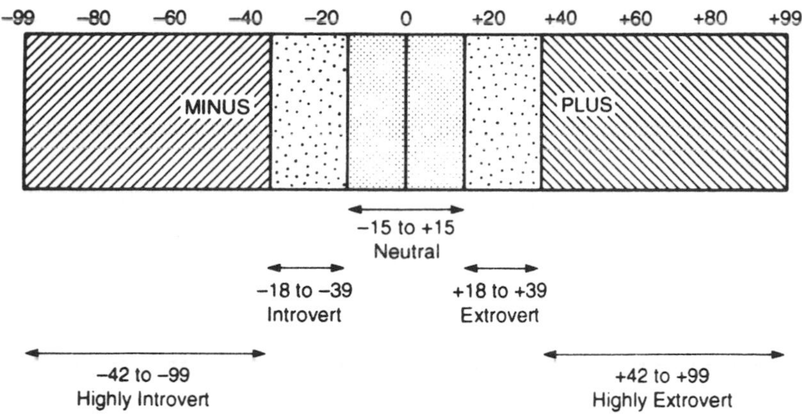

4 1–2–3 PROFILE

There are three ways of arriving at your direct reports' 1–2–3 profiles: you can either guess it yourself; hold a meeting where you discuss the concept and invite everyone to guess everyone else's profile; or you can invite your people (individually or collectively) to take the test. You should know from the feel of your team which route would be best for it to take.

Again, knowing the 1–2–3 profile is important for your direct reports for the same reasons as it is important to you: so that they can modify their job to trade on their area of strength and so that they can form 1–2–3 triumvirates wherever possible as effective sub-teams (see page 91).

5 THREE KEY DEVELOPMENT AREAS

Now think carefully about the three things that the individual needs to do to improve his or her performance and potential. These need not be remedial in nature, although clearly if the person has a skill improvement programme, those development needs should figure here. If, on the other hand, the person is quite competent in discharging current responsibilities, it is usually far better to concentrate on building up strengths and making them relevant to the team's work, than it is correcting weaknesses in the hope of building up an all-round, all-purpose executive.

People are naturally unbalanced: and thank heavens they are or it would be a very boring world. The majority of people spend their working lives suppressing and constraining their idiosyncrasies, with the result that they become progressively less creative at (and less happy with) their work. The fortunate few are those who deliberately mould their jobs and working lives to suit their own inclinations and capitalise on them. Hence self-employed people are often happier than those in large, monolithic corporations.

There is, however, no inevitability about the suppression of self that often takes place. It simply need not happen. It is a social phenomenon, not an economically necessary one. In fact, as the success of fledgling companies from Silicon Valley in California has demonstrated, the liberation of people's abilities from normal corporate constraints can prove enormously successful.

You should therefore encourage your people to build on their peculiar strengths, and you should think of ways in which you can shift your business domain and its mission in order to capitalise on these strengths.

6 INDIVIDUAL AND TEAM ROLES

You also need to think long and hard about the way that the strengths of your individuals can be combined and fused into an effective team, and into sub-teams. The way to balance strengths and weaknesses is not to generate a production line of well-rounded individuals, but to build a team out of unbalanced but complementary individuals, each of whom, as far as humanly possible, should spend the majority of their time doing things that they are proficient at and like. This does not happen most of the time and it does not happen automatically. It is your responsibility – and this is a creative task of a high order – to ensure that it happens as much as possible. Only you can do this. Your direct reports cannot choreograph the team as a whole. Your bosses do not have the time or the data or the responsibility. If you don't do it, no one will. And if you don't do it, you will not be extracting the maximum from your team or putting the maximum into it either. Everyone will lose in terms of productivity and happiness. So don't go home until you are well on the way to sorting this out.

7 HOW CAN THEY HELP YOU?

By now you should have come to conclusions that will eventually make huge improvements in the quality of working life and output of each of your key people. Now is the time to consider asking for something in return.

As the final part of your reflection on each individual, therefore, make a list of the three most important ways in which that individual can improve your own effectiveness.

It is amazing how few bosses stop to do this explicitly. Even those who do it implicitly often feel slightly ashamed or at least diffident about it. In case any such feelings cross your mind, let me tell you straight: there is no more important contribution any of your people can make than to help you to do your job better. Put crudely, your job is more important than theirs (otherwise there should not be a 'boss' position). You have been put in your job for a reason. You are the team leader responsible for getting the most out of the team. This is a difficult and tremendously important job.

So anything which can help you be more effective should be arranged and you should not be shy about requiring it. If it means that your direct reports need consequentially to spend less time on another less important matter (or to delegate it completely), so be it. Do not think it is an appropriate courtesy for you to let your people get on with their jobs without demanding very much of them to help you in theirs. Far from being a courtesy, it is a lack of imagination and boldness that ultimately harms everyone.

Creating the team

You should now be equipped with a little file on each of your key people which includes at least seven pieces of paper (or PC entries), one for each of the topics above. The next step is for you to sit down with each person and discuss your preliminary views with them, and work out action plans to help improve their individual effectiveness and contribution to the team.

In doing this, be fully humble and creative.

Humility is important because in thinking about people, you may have the wrong end of the stick. All of the comments and tests above are intended to provoke thought and offer possible ways forward, but they are not fully 'scientific' or infallible. (Actually, nothing is. Fortunately, capturing and classifying the human spirit is impossible. Generating insight into people is far more of an art than a science.) You might make mistakes about someone's attributes. You might also misinterpret signals from the person. So, when discussing any of the issues above, start out by being tentative and asking questions. When you wish to offer an insight of your own, always qualify it by saying something like, 'I don't know you very well yet, but my impression is . . .', rather than issuing *ex cathedra* statements that brook no possibility of contradiction. This way you will start a more constructive dialogue, as well as correcting much misleading data.

But also be creative. A 'counselling' or 'career development' session should be as relaxed and open ended as possible. It should not be a recital of prepared positions with a fixed outcome desired. Many of the best insights about how to make individuals and teams more effective arise spontaneously in discussion, rather than from solitary contemplation. Such insights will be strangled at birth (or before) if the atmosphere is at all highly charged or if the person feels forced on to the defensive. You must show flexibility and be prepared to change your views 'in real time'. The best outcome will arise if you are both stretching creatively for a win/win solution that will benefit all three parties: the individual, you and the whole team.

Remember to amend your own notes as a result of such sessions. Note carefully any commitments or actions that are to follow.

After all the discussions, you should have a team meeting to let everyone know any changes in responsibilities, what should be expected from each team member and how the team should help each other.

If you do this sensitively and enthusiastically, you are well on the road to recreating the team and making work fun for all those around you.

The day 40 checklist

1 Have you compiled for each of your key people a file addressing all of the seven points discussed above

Tick

A Yes ☐

B No ☐

2 Have you had discussions on similar lines with each of your key people?

A Yes ☐

B No ☐

3 Were the discussions open ended and constructive?

A Yes ☐

B Mainly ☐

C Not Really ☐

4 Did you modify some of your important views as a result of the discussions?

A Yes ☐

B No ☐

5 Do you honestly feel that it is now more 'your team' than 'the team I inherited'?

A Yes ☐

B To some degree ☐

C Not really ☐

6 Has the experience of the last two weeks identified significant ways in which you can do your own job better, with the help of your team?

A Yes, definitely ☐

B To some degree ☐

C Not really ☐

7 Do you feel that your team members are giving you straight answers to straight questions, or is there still a degree of inscrutability and/or game playing?

A There is still some game playing, but it is decreasing ☐

B There is still a lot of game playing ☐

C We are well past that stage; I think we are sharing feelings in a very straightforward way ☐

8 Is team morale higher or lower than when you came in as boss?

A I don't really know/probably little change ☐

B If I am honest, lower ☐

C I feel confident it is higher ☐

SCORING YOUR ANSWERS

Questions 1 and 2

For **each** A, score 10 points
For **each** B, score 0

Question 3

For A, score 10 points
For B, score 5 points
For C, score 0

Question 4

For A, score 10 points
For B, score 0

Questions 5 and 6

For **each** A, score 15 points
For **each** B, score 5 points
For **each** C, score 0

Questions 7 and 8

For **each** A, score 5 points
For **each** B, score 0
For **each** C, score 15 points

INTERPRETING YOUR SCORES

75–100 points Fantastic! Now build a periodic review along similar lines into your plans for the future. Keep your finger on the 'team pulse' at all times, rather than feeling that you have 'done that' and can get back to the business itself.

50–70 points Yes, I know it's difficult! You may have got higher scores on earlier checklists: this one is more testing. I know it takes a long time but it is worth the effort. Delay moving on until you reach at least 75 points.

0–45 points The breakthrough needed with your team is eluding you. Think whether you need a new approach. Go through the steps in this chapter again, and do not move on until you score at least 75 points.

7

Creating early success

The importance of early success cannot be overestimated. New leaders thrive on success and so do teams with a new leader. People elsewhere in your firm and in other organisations with which you deal frequently will tend to make snap judgements based on first impressions.

You can leave whether all this happens to chance – but there is an alternative, which is to engineer your clear early successes. In other words, you can create something that your team can feel proud of, and that will come to the attention of wider public opinion inside and outside your firm. Sometimes success happens spontaneously, but it is much safer to nudge it along a little. Or, as Gary Player remarked, 'I find that the more I practise, the luckier I become.'

Your task for the next ten days is to lay the groundwork for at least one clear, early success, which must happen within the next three months.

You will need a measure of cunning and calculation. Some hints may help here.

Pick the success arena carefully

The most important step is the first one: deciding which

area (or areas) to go for. Give this a great deal of reflection. Your objective should be to pick the area which will clearly qualify as a 'success', with the minimum amount of team effort and the minimum risk of failure. We will consider both halves of this proposition.

The clear success must be an achievement satisfying the following criteria:

- it must be something the team would feel is an achievement, something never previously attained and which would make the team feel good
- it must be a worthwhile task in itself, which would be of real benefit to people outside your unit
- it must be something that could come to the attention of people who are important to your unit, both inside and outside the firm. (It is OK if the 'coming to attention' requires some effort on your part in terms of propaganda or PR, as long as this is not too obviously 'hyped'.)

Remember that it should take **the minimum effort and risk of failure.** Hopefully you have been able to think of at least two or three clear successes that you could attempt. Now is the time to be ruthlessly practical in thinking which of these possible successes could be attained by the team most certainly and easily. It is better to go for a more modest objective (as long as it satisfies the three criteria above and is a genuine success) if it has a significantly better chance of happening than something more ambitious and risky.

The targeted **success** could be anything: to win an important new customer; to improve quality or service in a measurable and important way; to win an award; to hit a new level of monthly sales or profits; to get out of a costly and embarrassing mistake made by your predecessor; to launch a new product successfully; or anything else at all.

It is, of course, all the more impressive to do what others have proclaimed impossible. Usually this will involve doing something radical and smarter, rather than simply trying harder. You and your team should be able to think of something appropriate.

Whether or not you have the winning idea, make sure that the full team is involved in selecting it and that the team has a full opportunity to put forward other possibilities.

The pros and cons of spreading your bets

One way to facilitate success is to spread your bets, much like the old lady who backs every horse in a race in order to be sure of cheering home the winner. In terms of your work, this means selecting a number of potential early successes and working on them simultaneously in the hope that at least one will romp home. The downside, of course, is that effort will be dissipated among a number of projects and none of them will receive the critical mass of support to ensure success.

Use your common sense in deciding whether to go for one or more efforts. The only general hint is that if you can use different parts of your team to work on different efforts, this may be a sensible thing to do. If you go down this road, however, be sure to engineer things so that the whole team will feel and share in the success. If you cannot engineer this, or if using different parts of your team for different 'bets' is not feasible, it will probably be better just to concentrate on one objective and utilise all resources to make it happen.

Ensure you are leading the charge

Make sure that the chosen early success is something that you can make a noteworthy personal contribution towards. Then ensure that you do! Nothing inspires a team more than to see the leader revelling in the heat of the battle and being a practical help. But conversely . . .

Make sure that the team gets the credit

Never mention your own contribution. Instead, single out as many team individuals as you can for praise, both during the battle and after it has been won. Stress that it was a real team effort and just the precursor of many victories to come.

How to exceed expectations

The best way to exceed expectations is if there aren't any or if they are as low as possible at the start. So, although you should get the team excited about the challenge being tackled, you should wherever possible not tell anyone outside the team: not your boss, not others in the firm outside your unit, not the outside world. Otherwise you run the risk of attaining your goal, only to be met with a loud yawn from those who ought to be impressed. So tell your team to keep the task under wraps.

If outsiders do come to hear of what you are doing (and they may well do so), play down the probability of success and emphasise that it is a long, hard battle. Then you will still have the element of surprise and approbation when you triumph.

What if the team gets bogged down

It may be that you select a target with high hopes of success, but that after a week or two it is apparent that the nut is harder to crack than you all believed. In this case, do not persevere. It may well be that when the going gets tough, the tough get going, but that is usually because the tough are not very smart. However much the tough get going, they are only likely to dig themselves further into the hole.

The point was to select a quickly attainable target. If it turns out that this may well be a mirage, junk that objective (for the time being) and select another.

Because this is always a possibility, it's a good idea to have a substitute goal in reserve from the start, at least in your own mind.

What to do if you fail

It is possible, of course, that you may spend three months pursuing a goal you all believe is realisable, but then (through miscalculation, bad luck or simply inadequate execution) fail to crack it. It's too late to choose another target in the timescale. What do you do then?

Nil desperandum should be your watchword. Don't worry. Attaining the goal would have been a plus; not attaining it need not be a minus, unless you make it so. However frustrated or disappointed you are, do not let it show. Even in defeat, point out any positive things that have been achieved (if you look hard enough, these nearly always exist, even if they are only things like recognition that X is an unrewarding avenue of effort or the binding effect of working together as a team).

Focus the efforts of the team on another challenge, for there is nothing magic about the three-month goal. Always remember: the glass is not half empty; it is half full. And in some ways it really is more gratifying for a team to succeed the second or third time around than the first, and this would certainly make it easier to guard against arrogance or complacency after the victory.

How to celebrate success

Success, when it comes, should be sweet. Make sure that the team celebrates it with the right amount of gusto and panache. Remember that work should be fun, and if it can't be fun after you have scored a major success, when can it be? So be willing to set aside time and money for celebration – you will get a very good return on this investment. Take everyone out for a meal. Have a party. If the rest of the firm and the outside world has not noticed the achievement, they get another chance to learn about it if they see you and your people in festive mood: they are likely to ask why!

We human beings are pretty primitive animals. No matter what they say, everyone loves recognition, everyone loves flattery and everyone loves positive reinforcement. Therefore: recognise, flatter, reinforce. It is easier to do each of these in the wake of a signal victory.

Reinforcement is easier if you establish certain rituals (pleasant ones) which invariably follow team achievements. These may be relatively modest ones, such as buying doughnuts or small presents; or involve a little more expense, such as opening a few bottles of wine or champagne. It is a good idea to get into a regular ritual routine, if only because everyone will be looking out for the next success to justify another round of ritual.

But one word of warning. Do not let your team become over-confident, arrogant or complacent. Keep them on their toes with a fresh target 'success'.

And coming next . . .

Hopefully you have enjoyed planning for the team's first major success. Your task for the next two weeks will be equally necessary but not quite as much fun, for we are going to look at how to anticipate problems which will (not 'may'!) arise in the future. In the mean time, however, fill in the day 50 checklist and then have a recreational weekend.

The day 50 checklist

1 Will your chosen success area(s) add real value to the outside world and be regarded by your team as a real collective achievement?

Tick

A I haven't yet selected the success area(s), as I want to get it right, and I need more time to do this ☐

B Yes to both points ☐

C Yes to one point ☐

D No, but I want to start with a modest goal I am sure we can attain ☐

2 How many success areas have you chosen?

A Only one ☐

B 2 or 3 ☐

C 4 or more ☐

D As I said, I haven't chosen it/them yet ☐

3 Are you planning to play an important role in the task chosen yourself?

A No, it will be more motivating if others have bigger roles and therefore get the praise ☐

B Yes ☐

4 Have you publicised the task you are attempting outside your team, to increase the notice taken and the team's motivation?

A Yes ☐

B No ☐

5 Will you persevere if you get bogged down in the first few weeks?

A Yes ☐

B No ☐

6 What will you do if the team fails to realise the target?

A Nothing ☐

B Select another target ☐

C Forget about it ☐

D Conduct an investigation into why failure occurred, so we can learn from our mistakes ☐

7 Assuming that you are successful, will you highlight everyone's individual role in accomplishing the target?

A No, this would be divisive and demoralising for those who have not made a major contribution; I will praise the team as a whole ☐

B Yes ☐

C I will highlight the individuals who have made the greatest contribution, excluding myself ☐

8 Will you have a celebration after victory?

A Yes ☐

B No ☐

9 What two dangers are to be avoided after victory?

[Write down your answers and then see in the scoring section if you are correct]

SCORING YOUR ANSWERS

Question 1

Score 0 for A

Score 10 points for B

Score 0 for C or D

Question 2

Score 10 points for A or B

Score 0 for C or D

Questions 3, 4 and 5

Score 0 for **each** A

Score 10 points for **each** B

Question 6

Score 0 for A

Score 10 points for B

Score 0 for C or D

Question 7

Score 0 for A

Score 5 points for B

Score 10 points for C

Question 8

Score 10 points for A

Score 0 for B

Question 9

The correct answers are 'Arrogance' and 'Complacency'

Score 10 points for **each** of these answers

INTERPRETING YOUR SCORES

75–100 points Splendid! Give yourself a special treat this weekend.

50–70 points You clearly fell for at least one of the trick answers! Reread the chapter and then press on.

0–45 points Hmm. You didn't get the hang of this at all Wait until you are in a more receptive mood and then try again.

8

Spotting trouble ahead

By now you may be taking a slightly cynical view of this guide book. 'All this stuff about creating early successes is all very well,' you may be muttering, 'but it's as much as I can do to keep my head above water on a day to day basis. What help or advice can you give me to keep afloat?'

Well, in the words of Lynn Anderson, 'I beg your pardon, I never promised you a rose garden.' One of the bitter-sweet delights of leadership is facing adversity squarely in the face and facing it down, by maintaining a serene calm and optimism in the face of all evidence that the apocalypse is about to strike. So remember all the cheerful clichés your memory can dredge up – you know, things like 'If you can keep your head, when all around are losing theirs', 'The glass is not half empty, it's half full', 'Always look on the bright side of life' and so on – and rejoice in adversity. You're paid to deal with problems, so you might as well enjoy it. All the best epic stories spend at least as much time with the hero negotiating unforeseen danger as pursuing planned successes, so you're in good company.

But this chapter isn't exactly about dealing with evident difficulties. It's more about anticipating future problems. Now you may be groaning rather than muttering: you will already have been confronted by a string of crises and have put out some nasty fires, so the last thing you feel like doing is looking for trouble where none now exists.

But the trouble that's out in the open at an early stage has a more virulent brother: the trouble that's lurking with guile in the undergrowth, nourishing itself while weakening your defences, and ready to strike when you are at your most vulnerable and least prepared.

There are two corollaries from this. One is that you really should be pleased when troubles confront you in your first 100 days, because there's one less snake lying hidden in the tall grass and because you cannot really be held responsible for things that surface when you've only just started as boss. The other corollary is that you should literally go looking for trouble, and think carefully about what could go wrong in the future, so that you can head the trouble off and also be mentally prepared for the forces of evil.

The leader's job is to anticipate hidden trouble before it strikes. It comes in four distinct flavours, which are worth thinking about separately and systematically:

- internal trouble (within the team)
- intra-firm trouble
- trouble with customers and clients
- trouble from competitors.

We shall deal with these in turn.

Internal trouble

We talked in Chapter 6 about assessing the current team and creating the future team, and in Chapter 7 about facilitating team successes. But you can't just deal with these subjects for a few weeks and then forget them. All the time you will need to deal with your people and their issues, observe how well or otherwise the individuals and the team collectively are working, and think ahead about potential problems.

Do not worry so much about people who make their feelings evident, since you will already have been confronted with their concerns and (I trust) dealt with them. Instead, focus your antennae on the quieter individuals, those who are backward about coming forward.

Make time to have a personal chat with each of these people, starting with a real work topic, but seeking to elicit emotional as well as rational responses. Be sensitive to any underlying concerns, about their ability to do what is asked of them, about the pressures on them from outside and inside (and especially from you!), about whether what they are doing is useful, or about what their team role is and how they interact with the other team members.

Try to choose a time that is relatively quiet and free from interruptions from colleagues to have these discussions. It is best if the time selected shades gently from or into 'social' time, such as very early in the day before most people arrive (if dealing with an early riser), or at the end of the day, or (if you can escape from the crowd) at lunch. Alternatively, do it away from the office, on the business trip, or on some social occasion. Any of these tactics will facilitate a relaxed and more open talk. Be as natural as you can, and do not push for a heart to heart, person to person chat if none is needed or wanted: it may be intimidating rather than liberating.

Be as reassuring and positive as you can honestly be. Accentuate the positive. Praise a recent action. Make it clear that the person is a valued member of the team – you should honestly be able to do this, because if he or she isn't you should have exported them by now. Touch upon areas where the person knows more than you do, or has special skills on which you rely. (But do this in a light and natural way: there is nothing worse than someone feeling they have been deliberately buttered up or manipulated. Do not say anything you don't believe, but err on the side of generosity.) If you find it necessary in response to questions to offer some negative feedback, do it sandwiched between positive comments and take particular care to criticise specific actions, not the person themselves.

By the end of this fortnight you should have spoken along these lines to all your direct reports with whom you have not previously had a similar conversation, and to any of your other key people who are quiet and reserved. You will then have greatly improved your chances of heading off trouble from within the team.

Intra-firm trouble

This is potential trouble within the firm but outside the team, that is, with other departments or divisions. It is a sad fact that in many firms it is easier to co-operate with the outside world or even deal directly with competitors, than it is to deal with interdependent colleagues in a different discipline or place. The reason is the same one that generates conflict within families, or internecine struggle between sects or political parties of fairly similar persuasions: the competition for resources within a finite pool, for domestic space or people or money. Proximity often breeds aggression: because of the common link, it is felt that the normal courtesies extended to strangers or remote contacts can go by the board, or demands made which would seem unreasonable if made outside the fold.

In certain firms I have known (and often ones thought of

by the outside world as successful and professional), a majority of senior executives' time goes into political manoeuvring and internal battles, and only a minority into serving customers or beating competitors. This is a tragedy where it happens, and if you are in a firm like this my only advice to you is to foment a revolution, or if, as is probable, this would not succeed, either seek a management buy out of your unit or else look for another job in a better directed company.

So let's be quite clear that I am not advocating a cynical or Machiavellian approach to intra-firm politics. Your job is to ensure that your team spends as little time as it can on disputes within the firm, consistent with the team discharging its proper functions (some functions, such as quality control, or compliance, would not be doing their jobs properly without a certain amount of constructive tension). But minimising intra-firm conflict does not mean a Canute-like policy or the naïvety of 'see no evil, hear no evil, speak no evil'. On the contrary: it means vigilance, intelligence and resolute action.

Gifted leaders overcome the natural tendency towards unconstructive intra-firm conflict by focusing attention on the common company goal, and on common external enemies, and you should do this as much as possible for the people in your unit.

But other bosses in your firm may not be doing this fully. You can therefore expect trouble with colleagues outside your unit, especially from those that you most depend on or that most depend on your team. Here are some hints for how to anticipate the problems and resolve them.

STUDY THE FORM BOOK

Get a history of where conflict has arisen in the past, why

and what happened: the issues involved, how they were resolved and what points remain in dispute or uncomfortable. Think about whether, with hindsight, the matters fought over were really important or could have been settled more amicably. Reflect also on how any matters not tied up satisfactorily are likely to re-emerge as bones of contention.

WHAT CAN YOU DO

Next, think about what you and your team can do now to head off further trouble or remove the underlying cause of conflict. Decide, for each of the problem areas, which points could be dealt with fairly painlessly by changing the way your unit operates; which could be solved by additional resources; and which really do require a change in the way the other unit behaves. You may be surprised by how many fall into the first two categories. Corrective action is certainly in your control for the first category and it may well be for the second category too. Take whatever action you can here at once.

WHAT YOU NEED OTHER UNITS TO DO

To settle the third category of problems you will need help from the other unit (with which there has been trouble). Prepare yourself carefully and then go to talk to your opposite number in the other unit. Give your analysis on the causes of conflict, giving the other unit the benefit of the doubt where possible and taking on blame where appropriate for your unit's behaviour (when doing this, do *not* blame your predecessor but assume the blame yourself even if it's not justified). Say what you are prepared to do to smooth things over and then ask whether it would be possible for the other team to do X or Y in return.

THINK OF THE INTERESTS OF THE FIRM AS A WHOLE

Your rationale in such discussions and your touchstone throughout should be what is in the interest of the firm as a whole, not in the interests of your particular unit, and in particular not what will give your team an easy life. You may be surprised at being given advice to subordinate your unit's interests to those of the firm as a whole. What about all the books that tell you that business is all about power, that you should aggrandise your empire and polish its mystique, that you should keep bosses and other 'barons' at bay, and make yourself as powerful as possible by grabbing all available spare corporate resources?

The answer is that those days are going. It probably won't work today, unless you are in one of those awful firms referred to above, where in-fighting takes precedence over out-fighting. And even if it could work, it shouldn't. This is not the way of the market, not the way of value for money, but the old way of producer power and vested interests, and not the way of job satisfaction either.

Increasingly, those who run all organisations (and not just in the private sector) are insisting on 'seeing through' to the effect for the customer or client of actions taken by units within the organisation, to understand what is happening at each level, to eliminate waste, and to provide quality and value. More and more boards are realising the absurdity of pay and job evaluation systems that reward the boss for the number of subordinates, or the costs under his or her control.

This is a sensible trend which you should support rather than resist, partly because it is right, partly because it offers you and your team greater job satisfaction, and partly because it is the way to get on. If you are ambitious, the way to the top is to anticipate the time that you will be there; to start making decisions that are good for the company as a whole; to make it clear that you are taking a company-wide perspective. When promotion decisions are taken, it will be easier for the decision makers to imagine you in the new role. As often in life, long-term, enlightened self-interest can coincide with what is right and proper. It is only those trapped within their current roles who need to fight their corner regardless of everyone else.

Where possible, construct a simple cost benefit analysis of the points at issue or think of the profit implications of any step to remove the conflict. In some cases, the tension between two departments may be an inevitable and healthy stewardship of two legitimate interests, both of which help the firm.

For example, it is quite normal to have a tension between manufacturing, who want to produce as efficiently and at as low a cost as possible, and sales, who want to meet special customer requirements even if it means extra expense. The solution here is to work out whether the extra cost can be recovered in a higher price, and/or whether meeting special customer requirements can lead to much higher volume, which in turn enables average unit costs to be cut back to the original level because of greater spreading of fixed overheads. If so, sales are right and manufacturing, far from resisting customising, should be pleased, because it will lead to greater volume, market share and profit, and greater long-term manufacturing efficiency. But, equally, sales will then be on the hook to deliver the promised price and/or volume increases.

DO NOT COMPROMISE IF YOU ARE RIGHT

In 1984, Imperial Foods Limited, a diversified British food manufacturer, was considering whether to introduce a whole new range of low calorie, lower fat and lower salt products in canned foods such as baked beans, in crisps and in frozen ready meals. The marketing director argued for the changes in order to increase volume, but was unwilling to commit himself to specific numbers for the sales increases possible, arguing that the 'markets' to be served were embryonic and it was impossible to calculate how much demand could be created, how much would be cannibalised from the firm's existing products and how much siphoned off from competitors. The production director argued that the demand would probably be quite low, and that the changeover times for new products and the stock holding cost would be high. No numbers were actually calculated, and the matter was decided by which director had the stronger personality and greater clout in the board room.

This was the production man. As a result, the food manufacturer decided not to introduce the 'healthier' products. Different competitors in canned foods (Crosse & Blackwell, Heinz), crisps (led by the supermarket chain's own label suppliers, including United Biscuits) and frozen foods (Nestlé) made the leap in the dark, some of them after consumer research panels and careful analysis of break-even volumes. Almost a decade later, it is clear that the innovators were right, and that Imperial Foods made the wrong decision.

There are two morals from this story. The first is to be sure to conduct some analysis and research to establish the potential profit implications of any move. Even where the outcome is highly uncertain, analysis is useful to indicate what you have to believe in order to justify any action. Secondly, if you think you are right (and have some facts to support you), stick to your guns and argue what is in the firm's overall best interests. You should avoid unnecessary conflict, but not avoid necessary conflict. But keep the argument focused as far as possible on profit for the firm.

Despite the above advice on 'necessary conflict', the result of you anticipating intra-firm conflict should be to greatly diminish its overall level. If this does not happen in the next few weeks, the odds are that you are doing something wrong.

Trouble with customers and clients

Your unit may have external customers, but even if it does not, it will have clients, those who should benefit from what the unit is doing (if it does not have clients, it should not exist).

The first step is to define who exactly your customers and clients are. It is a good idea to divide these into the core group and the secondary group. Some customers and clients are more important than others. These, the core group, are your 'loyal', regular, dependable customers. By definition, they are bound to you because they generally depend on your product or service: either because it is in their opinion better than any alternative (in terms of quality, value, service or convenience) or because, in the short run, they have little or no choice (as may be the case with an in-firm client).

It is absolutely essential that you know what your core customers'/clients' **hot buttons** are – the things that really excite them to joy or anger. So talk to them, face to face, using the opportunity of being new in your job to find out how satisfied they are, what they like about the unit's product and service, and how, in their view, it could be improved.

You will soon find that although all customers are different and want to be treated individually, most of them fall into a small number of groups, each of which has a lot in common with fellow group members and much less in common with customers in other groups. In marketing jargon, these separate groups of customers are called segments (although most marketing theory tries to give you ready-made segments based on social class or life-style, which are about as useful as lightweight clothes in a blizzard).

For useful comments on how to find and use hot buttons and segments, you may want to refer back to Chapter 3, especially pages 53–59 and 62–63. Now is the time to make sure that you have identified all your core customers, that you know which segment each belongs to and that you know which are the most important 'purchase criteria' or hot buttons for each customer.

At this stage you may ask, isn't this chapter about avoiding trouble? Aren't we confusing downside avoidance with upside potential? The answer is: No! When it comes to customers (especially core customers), the best and only defence is attack. You will lose customers and market share (real or psychological) if you do not provide what they want. So do not wait until they grumble or (far worse) vote with their feet. Take the initiative in keeping them happy; in this case, the only way to avoid the down-side is to pursue aggressively the upside.

You will now want to create an action programme to improve the hold you have on each of the core customers and if possible to raise the value of what they buy from you. Bill Bain, the head of the fastest growing and most profitable management consultancy of the 1980s, Bain & Co., used to sell bibles door to door in the US deep south, and recounted how he went for miles and miles knocking on doors, vainly trying to find new customers, before he realised that the best prospects for a new sale were his existing customers. He then (so he said) built a successful practice on selling another bible to his core customers.

Selling more to your existing core customers can be achieved in three ways: either by providing extra quality or service on the existing product offering, and so raising, price; and/or by selling greater quantities of the existing products (by offering price concessions or other benefits, in return for a greater share of their business); and/or by selling completely new products. Think laterally with your team about how any of these approaches could be used to generate new business.

Then agree who is to do what by when to win additional business for core customers. Set up a monitoring system to see how it is going.

Then, and only then, move on to consider the secondary clients and customers. How can they be converted into core clients? The methods to be used are the same as for core clients, but be more selective and focus on those which you and the team judge to have the greatest upside potential.

Finally, under this heading, move on to consider completely new customers and clients. There may not be time to do this in the ten days under review. If not, schedule a careful review of new customer opportunities for some time in your second 100 days.

Trouble from competitors

Just as all units have customers or clients, so all units have competitors, external, internal or both.

Step 1 is to identify who they are. Companies are often remarkably unaware of their true competition. If it varies from one area of business to another, divide the business up into these areas (incidentally, this is often a very sound basis on which to structure the internal organisation and customer marketing efforts) and do not rest until each area has identified its most important competitors (usually, the top three or five or ten). If you are in doubt as to who your most serious competitors are, ask yourself the following questions:

- Who do we meet most often in pitching for new business?
- To whom have we lost market share?
- Who scores as high as us or higher in surveys of our customers?
- Who in my business area would I most like to go to work for, if I decided to jump ship?
- Who provides the product or service most directly comparable to our own?

Having identified your competitors, step 2 is to identify objectively where they are better than you and where they are worse. Use customer survey material and any reliable measures of performance that are available. Think in terms of segments: which groups of customers do they have most appeal to and which least? Step 3 is to find out the market share held by each competitor in each segment and compare it to your own market share in that segment.

Relative market share is much more important and useful

a measure than absolute market share. For example, you might have a 10 per cent market share in Segment A and a 15 per cent market share in Segment B, and therefore conclude that you have a stronger position in the latter segment. But what if your major competitor, the Bare Fangs Corporation, has a market share of only 5 per cent in Segment A but a 30 per cent share in Segment B? (Assume also that no third player has a larger share of the market in either case.) It should be intuitively apparent that, relatively speaking, you are in stronger position in Segment A than in Segment B, despite your higher absolute share of Segment B.

Why is this? Given a free choice, twice as many Segment A customers pick you over Bare Fangs, whereas the reverse is true in Segment B. Because of this preference, all other things being equal, you should be able to command a higher price than Bare Fangs in Segment A and Bare Fangs should be able to command a premium price in Segment B.

Additionally, you should be able to have lower costs than Bare Fangs in Segment A, because you can spread your fixed costs over greater volume. In Segment B, the same reason should give Bare Fangs a lower cost.

In this simple example, you should have a higher price and a lower cost than Bare Fangs in Segment A, and therefore much higher profit. For Bare Fangs, Segment B should give the same advantage.

If you just looked at your own market share, you might find it hard to understand why Segment A, where you have 10 per cent market share, should be much more profitable than Segment B, where you have a 15 per cent share. But if you looked at *relative* market share, you would be the leader in Segment A but a follower in

Segment B, which would explain the difference in profitability.

Relative market share can be quantified as being your segment share divided by the segment share of the largest competitor in the segment, or, if you are the largest competitor, your segment share divided by the share of the next largest competitor.

In this example, your relative market share of Segment A is your share divided by Bare Fangs' share, that is, 10 per cent divided by 5 per cent, i.e. 2 (usually expressed as '2x', 'two times', or '200 per cent'). Your relative market share of Segment B is 15 per cent divided by 30 per cent, i.e. 0.5 (usually expressed as '.5x', or 'point 5 times' or 50 per cent).

Conversely, Bare Fangs' relative market share in Segment A is 5 per cent divided by 10 per cent, or .5x, and in Segment B is 30 per cent divided by 15 per cent, i.e. 2x. As a rule of thumb, relative market share is an excellent indicator of competitive strength, and you should rank your segments in order of this measure. Again, as a crude guide, provided you have defined your segments properly (and not mixed together apples and pears, where you face different competitors):

- A relative market share of 1.5x or greater, i.e. where you are 50 per cent bigger than anyone else, indicates dominance (which is usually excellent news and where you should be obscenely profitable)
- A relative market share of 1x or greater, i.e. where you are segment leader, indicates a very strong position, where you should be very profitable
- a relative market share greater than 0.7x, but smaller than 1x, is a reasonably strong position

- a relative market share of 0.5x to 0.7x is a moderate, mediocre position
- a relative market share of less than 0.3x is weak and usually unprofitable.

It is easy to get misled by incorrect segmentation or data, but (unless your industry faces an unusual balance between demand and capacity, or is regulated) there is likely to be a strong correlation between your relative market share and your true profitability (which, again, may not be the profitability shown by your firm's accounting system). We should just mention in passing two further corollaries:

- if you are really very strong in a segment (in terms of relative market share) and it is not very profitable for you, the chances are that you have a major profit improvement opportunity, either by raising price, or by lowering your costs, or by both means
- if you are really very weak in your segment relative market share, and it is highly profitable, the chances are that these profits will not last, unless you make your position more secure by gaining market share.

'All this is very interesting,' you may be saying, 'but what are the action implications of all this stuff about relative market share?'

I'm glad you raised the question. There could be all sorts of implications, but most of them fall well outside the timescale of your first 100 days and the ambit of this book. For your immediate purposes, there are two key points:

- Concentrate on reinforcing and building up your very strong segments, where you are already in leadership positions and highly profitable. As this book keeps stressing, building on strength is by far the most rewarding approach. Think about how to raise volume, raise price, lower cost, eliminate competitors, and introduce new products and improved service and quality. Reinvest in success.

- Consider withdrawing from your weak (low relative market share and low profit) segments. Refocus your team's efforts away from these areas. Pay less attention to customers here. Raise prices and be relaxed if you lose business. Or, if possible, sell the business or give it to another part of your organisation more suited to deal with it.

Step 4 is to act on your insights and decisions. Be sure to make individual team members accountable for achieving results.

But what if you don't have external competition (the focus of this section from page 132)? If you are an internal cost centre providing a service to your organisation, you still have 'shadow' competitors who could conceivably do what your unit does. These 'shadows' might be other departments inside your company or third parties who could provide your service as external contractors. Large companies, central governments and local governments throughout the world are increasingly looking to external contractors as a way of improving value for money and making their jobs more manageable. If you can't think of potential 'shadows', this is almost certainly a failure of your imagination rather than because they don't exist.

So, identify the shadow competitors that could (perhaps with a moderate shift in strategy or resources) do what your unit is doing. You can now follow one of two strategies in relation to these 'shadows'.

One strategy is to ensure that your unit provides its service at much lower cost, or at a much higher level of quality and service, than any conceivable competitor could. You have to work out whether this is possible and how.

The alternative strategy, if you can't beat the 'shadows' in a fair fight, is to join them or, to be more precise, work out a plan for merging your unit into a shadow competitor or abolishing your unit and suggesting that the organisation contract out its work. This is, of course, a radical strategy, and not one that many of you are likely to adopt. You should, however, consider it seriously. In many cases, 'shadows' could do a far better or lower cost job than in-house units, because they have much higher volume and/or superior technology, or because they have a commercial motive to provide an excellent service.

To give one example, 20 years ago every large company had its own information technology unit, with its own computers, computer operators and systems engineers. Now there is a strong trend towards facilities management and support provided by large, expert companies, selling a total package of service to host companies, who are thereby able to free up capital and manpower, and concentrate on what they do best.

This sort of trend is or could be extended into a whole variety of other areas: human resources management, production management, contract sales forces, contract administration, contract security, contract transport fleet management, contract purchasing and so on: almost any service can be provided by a specialist, often at lower cost and/or to a higher standard.

Some would argue that the mid-21st-century corporation will focus exclusively on its area of core competence – say, marketing, or manufacturing, or research – and contract out the whole of the rest. There is a lot of economic logic behind this approach, although defining areas of competence may be increasingly elusive as interdisciplinary learning becomes the hallmark of the effective corporation. Such speculation would be irrelevant for your immediate purposes, except that it should serve as a buffer against complacency and a spur to providing 'captive' clients with at least as good a service as that provided to customers who are free to move easily between competing suppliers.

Another weekend ahoy!

Now all that stands between you and a reinvigorating weekend is our customary checklist test for day 60.

The day 60 checklist

1 Have you had a quality, personal discussion with each of your quieter direct reports about their aspirations, hopes and fears with regard to their job and their role in the team?

Tick

A Yes ☐

B Not to all, but to most ☐

C No, there hasn't been the time or opportunity yet ☐

2 Do you feel you have a good reading on how your team thinks about you and each other

A Yes ☐

B To some degree ☐

C Not really ☐

3 Have you given praise to your team members whenever praise is due?

A Yes ☐

B Most of the time ☐

C Probably not ☐

4 Have you identified specific problems with team members that may arise in the future?

A Yes ☐

B No ☐

5 Are you strenuously trying to extend your unit's size and power?

A Yes ☐

B No ☐

6 Have you identified specific problems with other parts of the organisation that may arise in the future?

A No ☐

B Yes ☐

7 Have you defined your core clients and customers

A No ☐

B Yes ☐

8 Do you have a rough idea of your relative market share in each important segment of your business?

A No ☐

B Yes ☐

9 If your market share in a segment is 40 per cent, your nearest competitor in that segment has 30 per cent, and your most important overall competitor has only 10 per cent in that segment, what is your segment relative market share?

A 1.33x ☐

B .67x ☐

C .25x ☐

D 4x ☐

E 1.5x ☐

10 What policy should you have towards part of your business that has a low relative market share but is very profitable?

A Milk it ☐

B Keep the position just as it is today ☐

C Place a low priority on it ☐

D Sell it if you can get a good price ☐

E You should be worried about it and look at it very carefully ☐

F Try to gain market share quickly ☐

SCORING YOUR ANSWERS

Questions 1, 2 and 3

Score 10 points for **each** A
Score 5 points for **each** B
Score zero for **each** C

Questions 5, 6, 7 and 8

Score 0 for **each** A
Score 10 points for **each** B

Question 9

Score 10 points for A
Score 0 for B, C, D or E

Question 10

Score 0 for A, B or C
Score 10 points for D, E or F

INTERPRETING YOUR SCORES

90–100 points	Another gold star
70–85 points	Make sure you can correct your minor mistakes in the next fortnight
50–65 points	Reread the chapter and put back your schedule by two weeks
0–45 points	A wooden spoon. I don't think I'm helping you much.

9

Focusing on profit

The topic for the next two weeks is nice and simple: profit. Although this is a short chapter it is one of the most important. The ideas may seem facile and obvious, but use the next two weeks to think carefully and often about whether you have really taken the ideas to heart and are putting them into daily practice.

What if you're not a profit centre?

You can still think about profit! Remember the simple equation:

Profit equals Price minus Cost times Volume

It then becomes clear that even if you have no responsibility for or impact on prices or revenues, you can still contribute to profits by lowering cost.

Costs can always be lowered. Twenty years ago it was fashionable to draw 'experience curves' which purported to show that costs should go down as volume and learning went up (as a function of something called 'accumulated experience', i.e. the number of units of a product or service ever produced). As a consultant I believed in the theory and would often come up with an apparently scientific finding that costs in this or that area could be lowered by

10 per cent or 20 per cent. My clients nearly always believed the finding and then were able to get their people to lower costs by the desired amount.

Later I joined another consulting firm and found that I had been misapplying the theory, and I came up with different (usually higher) amounts that costs could be cut by. Lo and behold, the costs were then reduced, sometimes by as much as 35 per cent.

The experience curve theory is not now held in such regard, which makes it more difficult to achieve the results. The approved theory is now called benchmarking and it, too, produces major cost savings.

My considered view (which is not cynical) is that if any group of managers truly believes that costs can be cut by a reasonable amount (say 20 per cent), then those costs can be cut, without damage to the business. Cost is a massively more variable thing than we generally believe. Cost expands to fill our expectation of what can be afforded and is generally only cut in times of crisis, when it is always possible. This is a major missed profit opportunity. Cost can be cut at almost any time, with a really measurable impact on profits.

Cutting costs should not be an across-the-board, miserable, miserly rote exercise. It should be a creative and fun project. Some questions to ask include the following:

- What has been the history of each cost element over time, both absolutely and as a percentage of sales? If we survived on X amount of total cost or Y per cent of sales five years ago, why do we need more now?
- How much would we lower unit cost if we raised volume by 50 per cent (i.e. what costs are really fixed, whatever the volume?). If we did this how much could we afford to

'give away' in lower prices, promotions, increased sales costs or better quality, in order to realise the volume increase?

- Do we do some things that we could simply stop doing, without any ill effects?
- Do we do some things that we could stop doing, provided we did something else (cheaper) instead?
- Can we make some of our costs lower in exchange for giving away a share of profits? Can this be done in a way that benefits everyone?
- If you personally owned the business, are there things you would do differently?
- If the business was independent of its parent, would costs be higher or lower? Is the parent really providing value for money?
- Are there creative ways of doing things totally differently that would lower costs dramatically at some time in the future, even if they cost money in the short term?
- How do we make sure that costs continue to be scrutinised and go down, bit by bit, month by month, after the current blitz on cost? How do we build in cost and value consciousness on the part of everyone, every day?
- Can we offer our people some share of the cost reductions achieved, either directly in pay or profit sharing, or indirectly by special treats or quality of working life?

If you are a cost centre, your impact on profits almost certainly extends beyond the cost side. It is probable that you do or could have a significant impact on the other two elements of profit: price and volume.

Price for most products and services varies by a greater

amount than is often appreciated. We still tend to believe in the defunct micro-economists' model of perfect competition, where everyone tends to have the same price, profit and cost. Empirical observation of any of these variables will contradict the theory.

As far as price is concerned, look for instance at the same goods available in different types of outlet. It is not uncommon to pay 30–40 per cent more for exactly the same product in a convenience store compared to a discount supermarket. Wander round a normal supermarket, and look at the difference between a premium brand and a number two or three brand (often 10–15 per cent difference) or between a premium brand and the supermarket own label product (often 25–40 per cent). These differences create enormous scope for differential profitability, for both retailers and manufacturers, on 'similar' products.

I have often calculated product line and outlet profitability for consumer goods manufacturers, and amazed both myself and them at the huge differences, where some categories earn 25 per cent return on sales and others make large losses. This creates large opportunities for profit improvement by steering a greater proportion of product into the higher profit categories. If this requires a bit more quality or service (or just calculation!) it is well worth it.

So the cost centre should have a major role in helping provide extra quality or service where it really pays off. Work out where these opportunities are.

There is a similar or greater opportunity on volume. Of the profit trinity, volume often has the greatest effect, because it influences profit three times: once in its obvious role of multiplying the profit margin by the numbers sold;

secondly through its effect over time on your cost; and thirdly in its effect on your competitors' volumes and costs. To adapt St Paul: 'Price, Cost and Volume, these three; but the greatest of these is Volume'.

Each cost centre should think hard about how it can help to raise volume. Building in better service and/or quality are clearly relevant again, but there may be other ways too. Cost centres are often in touch with customers, and should use every ploy and ounce of their intelligence to work out how sales could be increased. This might involve adaptation of the existing product, a premium service for part of the market, the introduction of a new product or service, or displacing a vulnerable competitor by a well-timed offer. The cost centre cannot make this happen, but can often be a valuable catalyst.

The rest of this chapter is for managers with even more direct profit responsibility.

Are you really focused on profit?

You may think you are, but is it really true? Check the list below.

LESS CAN BE MORE

Most people's instincts are to think that if business is expanding, things must be going well. The temptation to go for profitless growth is hard to resist, particularly as it never goes under its true colours. Profitless growth comes in many seductive flavours: the absorption of another unit or division; the expansion into another part of the value added chain (for example, a marketing company backward integrating into manufacture or a producer opening a shop); the development of expensive new products which go beyond the group's core skills; the American subsidiary (often a most engrossing cash sink); the alluring acquisition; and many more.

Think where you are, how you got there and whether (with hindsight) it was wise to get there. Remember that history can often be reversed, with clear thinking and vigorous action. Shared costs are often the excuse for not reversing something. But costs do not need to be shared and if you shed certain business, perhaps your fixed costs could get unfixed and be drastically slimmed to meet the needs of the retained business only. It is usually the case that all but the simplest businesses have a tail of unprofitable business, typically comprising 20–25 per cent of the total business. Think about whether this is true in your own case.

Do you know your product line profitability?

By product line profitability, I mean the fully costed profitability of each significant chunk of your business. Defined strictly, this means your return on sales and/or return on capital of each of your products.

More loosely, this can also include profitability by segment, wherever there are differences in the business that could give rise to differential costs, prices and profits. Particular customers may comprise a separate segment, or particular channels of distribution, or particular grades of product, or particular locations.

Most businesses are lazy and evasive about product line or segment profitability. Put bluntly, they don't know it. They may know intuitively that certain customers attain lower prices or have extra costs, but they usually underestimate the effects. Managers tend to argue that it is difficult and arbitrary to allocate overheads and fixed costs to products or certain sorts of businesses.

It may be difficult, it probably will be somewhat arbitrary, but do it! Every exercise on segment profitability I have ever seen has thrown up some surprising and useful results. If you do the analysis, there will be two important benefits:

- You will be able to see which business is most profitable. You can then take actions to ensure you hang on to it, and try to expand this and similar business.
- You will be appalled at how unprofitable some business is. You can then take corrective action, either by cutting it out and reducing costs accordingly, or by raising price, or by lower costs on this part of the business.

Are you thinking long term?

You should be planning for where you want the business to be in five or ten years' time. This is not just a matter of great leaps forward, but also a continuous process of improvement by tiny steps. Here are some points to consider:

- **Quality.** How can it be improved?
- **Service.** How can you make customers really happy?
- **Technology.** How can you shift gears through using different technology?
- **Volume.** What market share do you have now and what do you need to be a clear market leader? Is this feasible, either overall or in particular segments? Are you monitoring market share and relative market share by segment? Do you have early warning systems

that tell you if market share is being lost or is vulnerable?

- **People.** How do you get the best people available in your field and keep them?
- **Competition.** How do you make life difficult for competitors and get them in the habit of giving you a clear run?
- **Costs.** What should your units costs be next year, in five years, ten years? How can you start a continuous process of cost reduction and keep it up?
- **Prices.** How can you build relative price advantage, by having prices higher than competitors while not losing market share? How can you offer extra perceived value, by branding, service level or ingenuity, that gives you a higher price without incurring a commensurate increase in cost to you?

Are you investing enough?

You can always spend too much, but it is more difficult to invest too much. What is the difference between spending and investment?

Spending means that there is no residual benefit after a certain time period is up. Thus you can spend on higher pay, on employing more people, on a one-off promotion, or on the myriad forms of corporate overhead that prove so irresistible.

Investment means that there is a measurable and major benefit being built up over time, which should put a gap between you and competition in terms of quality, service or cost. It can be investment in a new generation of production equipment or information technology, in material technology, in brand image and identity, in your people's skills and abilities to manage change, in the organisation's ability to learn, in strategic alliances with other firms, or in anything else that will mean higher market share and profits in the future.

Pseudo-investment is spending on anything that does not reinforce competitive advantage in a tangible, definable, measurable way. The distinction between investment and pseudo-investment is whether or not it is likely to work. This can be a matter of judgement, even of faith. For example, decisions made by companies like Procter & Gamble in the 19th century and again in the Depression of the 1930s to offer security of employment could either have been investments or pseudo-investments, depending on whether there was a real payoff in terms of attracting the best people, retaining them and getting the most out of them, in ways which enhanced service to customers and efficiency. Most observers would judge that P&G and similar organisations made a good investment.

What is the constraint on growing profits?

Most of us do not give free rein to our imagination and tend to accept the hand we are dealt. One safeguard against this as a new boss is to ask, 'Why shouldn't my team double/triple/quadruple profits?' What's stopping you?

Imagine that you could have as much resource as you wanted – no artificial restrictions on people, on money available, or organisational barriers to what your team could do. The only requirement you would still need to fulfil is that your unit earned an adequate return on the money you tied up.

What could you do then? Don't worry if investment is necessary that would only pay off in five or ten years' time. Don't worry at this stage if it takes you well beyond the payback period the organisation allows or if it would involve 'unacceptable' dilution of earnings per share or other shibboleths.

If you really believe in it, decide to go for it. Then work out how to circumvent the corporate control systems. But be clear in your own mind first that you really are in it for the company's long-term profit and not for your own ego trip. If this really is true, you should be able to muster the enthusiasm and corporate vision to command the support of your colleagues.

You, profit and your team

This chapter has been addressed to you as boss, largely independent of your team. Your thinking about profit as you went about your business over these two weeks may therefore not have been shared at all with your team. This does not matter, as long as you now write down what you have learnt, what you suspect may be true, and what data and analyses you need in order to prove or disprove your hypotheses, and discuss all this with the team. You and they need to be profit minded all the time and if there are some loose ends still to be tied up after these two weeks (such as a careful look at segment profitability) that is no bad thing. It may also help to scan this chapter from time to time in the future, just to check that it is long-term profit you are pursuing.

The day 70 checklist

1 Name the three members of the profit trinity.

2 Which is the greatest and why?

3 Have you conducted a review of costs? How much do you think they can be cut?

4 Have you set steps in place to implement your cost cutting?

5 Do you know your rough product line and segment profitability? If not, are you gathering the data to tell you?

6 What is the difference between an investment on the one hand and a cost or pseudo-investment on the other?

7 Do you agree that the best route to profit improvement is through periodic reviews and the identification of great leaps forward?

8 Have you discussed your insights on profit with your team?

Note: We may have confused you by not offering multiple choice answers. This is because we think too many of you were guessing the answers to the previous checklists rather than thinking them out for yourselves. Covering the answers set out below, write your suggestions in the space provided or on a separate piece of paper and then score your answers.

SCORING YOUR ANSWERS

1 Price, cost and volume. Score ten points for **each** of these.
2 Volume. Because it has three effects on profit: the multiple effect, the effect on your costs and the effect on competitors. Score ten points if you got this approximately correct, or five points if you nominated volume but did not say why correctly.
3 The correct answer is **yes**, and by at least 20 per cent. Score ten points for this.
4 Score ten points if you can honestly say **yes**.
5 You are a very fast worker if you answered **yes** to the first question. Score ten points for a **yes** to either question.
6 An investment confers a real competitive advantage in the future. The difference is whether it works in practice. Score ten points for a similar answer.
7 The correct answer is **no.** As the Japanese know, profit improvement is best thought of as a continuous process of small steps, as a way of life. Great leaps forward have their place, but are not enough. Score ten points for **no.**
8 Not surprisingly, the right answer is **yes.** An alternative,

even better, answer is 'No, the insights came up during discussion with them in the first place.' Score ten points for either of these.

INTERPRETING YOUR SCORES

85–100 points I am running out of compliments. Your chances of completing the course with distinction look very good. Ensure that your insight is matched with action and that you remember to follow through.

70–80 points Not bad. Be sure you understand where you dropped points and why.

50–65 points Try again.

0–45 points You belong in an old style government bureaucracy.

10

Learning from failure

The value of setbacks

If you are doing your job properly you should have notched up some notable failures by now. Failures are the inevitable result of ambitious activity: if you do nothing challenging, you are unlikely to fail; but if you are attempting several difficult tasks, you are almost bound to fail at some of them. Failure is a vigorous sign of life and its value is rarely understood. For the next two weeks your off-line task is to think about the failures you have already experienced and may experience in the future, and reflect on your own and with your team about the value of failure.

Setbacks are valuable for three reasons. First, they contain precious data. Do it this way and you will fail; do it slightly differently and you may succeed. Reading these data is an art which few people master; those who do have a corresponding advantage. Failure puts you in touch with reality in a way that success cannot do. Negative feedback should be taken seriously. Your task is to become skilled at interpreting feedback and at training your team to do the same.

Secondly, although it a cliché, failures really do have the potential to be character building. Behind every great man or woman lies failure. Just as epic stories and novels must have their twists and turns, reversals of fortune can put you in touch with inner reality, the resilience that must come from within, the sense of self-worth, integrity and striving to perform. When things have gone badly, you are forced back on what you can do well, what you can contribute to other people and the world, to making the best of your skills and resources. On the other hand, a life of effortless success breeds complacency, arrogance and superficiality.

Thirdly, failure makes it easier to win allies. Few people like to be the junior partner in an alliance. People like to feel that you depend on them as much as they depend on you, preferably more. It may not be an attractive human trait, but we nearly all like to see successful people or companies slip on a banana skin from time to time. We tend to prefer the underdog to the overdog. And since corporate life, no less than the rest of life, depends more on what others can do for you than on what you can do for yourself, it is no bad thing to be cast in the role of gritty underdog, struggling against the odds to overtake a better placed rival.

The problem with failure is the stigma we all attach to it. Most of us thrive on success. Few of us thrive on failure. We think we cannot cope with too much of it, so we tend to deploy harmful defence mechanisms that blind us to the reality of failure. We brush failure aside, we refuse to think about it, we harden our hearts to the possibility that we may have been at fault and we project our failure on to another party (an option that is always available outside a monastery). Because we do all these things, failure ceases to be an irritant, but loses all its potential value. Denying failure is a mark of weakness, not of strength. You should take pride in your failures and your ability to learn from them.

Your ten best failures

Enough of this homily: let's get down to work. Make a list of your 10 'best' failures at work, including all the failures during your first 70 days as new boss. If you can't rack up ten such failures, go back in history to your last job too. By 'best' failures, we mean those that were failures on a big scale and/or failures that you think have the best potential to teach you something about yourself in a work context.

For each failure, write down its nature and its consequences. Then analyse the three most important reasons for the failure. Each reason should reflect a weakness on your part, in terms of judgement or action. You are not allowed to put down reasons like 'bad luck' or 'someone else's stupidity', since, even if true, these reasons (excuses?) do not allow you to learn very much. (But it would be valid to put down things like, 'Over-optimism on my part', or 'Relying on Mr X, who could not deliver what he promised'.) Next, attempt to state what conditions would have been necessary for success. Finally, for each failure put a letter code against it if any of the following were contributory causes to the failure and circle the most important letter code for each failure:

EO	Excessive optimism	Believing task would be much easier
HR	Human relations	Insufficient attention or skill in persuading others
ID	Insufficient data	Making a decision without the relevant facts
IF	Insufficient force	Not allocating enough resources to do job
IT	Insufficient training	Not equipping your team with tools for job

OD	Over delegation	Giving your team too much rope
PA	Poor analysis	Not thinking through what was important in accomplishing the task
PE	Poor execution	Right idea, but badly implemented
RA	Relying on allies	Trusting others (not your team) who did not deliver
WI	Wrong idea	Trying to do the wrong thing

You can list any number of these causes for each failure, but remember to circle the most important cause for each as well. If you want to invent new categories that are relevant to your work, go ahead.

At the bottom of your list, make a tally of the number of times each of these reasons for failures occurs and another tally of the number of times each reason was the most important (circled) cause.

You should now have a valuable profile of the most frequent mistakes you are making, as well as insight into the most valuable things that you could be doing differently, that would have been most likely to turn failures into successes.

Insight for the team

If you found this a helpful exercise, gather your team together at some time in this fortnight. If you have the nerve to do it, expose your own anatomy of failure to them (suitably edited if necessary!), and invite each of them to come up with their top three personal failures and their view of the whole team's top three failures since you took over, analysed in the same way.

Give your team members the option of revealing their own personal failures or not, but ask each person to list and discuss the team failures. Make sure that you conclude with steps that the whole team and particular individuals should take in order to reduce the incidence of future failure.

You may find that the team ends up discussing potential failures, that is, things which have not yet failed but which one or more team members fears may. This could become a very productive session, pinpointing ways to improve your chances of success.

External causes of failure

So far we have homed in on things that you and the team are doing to contribute to failure. In one way, you are always at fault and always have something to learn from failure. But there is an additional (not alternative!) useful way for the boss to look at failure, which examines the external, structural causes of failure. This is also a valid perspective. As you read the description below of five of the most important structural reasons, reflect on parallels with your own experience and on what can be done to avoid falling into the same traps.

1 FORCES OF REACTION

If you are trying to do something new, different from your predecessor's policy or the prevailing way of doing things, the odds are that you will provoke a reaction, perhaps even ferocious opposition, from one or more 'forces of reaction' that seeks to block your initiatives. The reactionaries may be inside or outside the company: your staff, your bosses, your peers, vested interests in the industry, competitors, regulators – anyone!

Your first task is to notice these forces of reaction. Do not deny their existence or importance, or they may ambush you in short order. Look for opposition at least as keenly as for support.

Secondly, assess objectively the strength of each element of the opposition, its real reasons for opposing change and its areas of weakness: identify its soft underbelly.

Thirdly, if there is more than one force of reaction, try to stop the different opposition forces from linking up with each other. If possible, keep them ignorant of each other's existence. If that is not possible, and the forces are potentially much more dangerous together, work out how to win round, buy off or rout the opposition that can be neutralised at least cost to you.

Fourthly, for any remaining opposition, decide your strategy. You have at least five options, any of which may be the best in the circumstances. These are: frontal attack; circumnavigation; compromise; capitulation; or biding your time.

- **Frontal attack** is advisable only if you are confident of victory or if the matter is such an important point of principle that defeat is preferable to compromise.
- **Circumnavigation** is often effective. This means not challenging the forces of reaction, and even appearing to concede the point, while then finding a way to achieve your goals through another route. For instance, you might agree not to use the salesforce to distribute your proposed new product, but start a direct mail campaign instead, perhaps by using outside contractors.

- **Compromise** is not to be spurned, especially if you can achieve most of your objectives while clothing them in the current ideology. Politicians make an art form of this. Macmillan withdrew from Suez while pursuing a hostile stance; Nixon did the same thing over Vietnam. Stalin claimed to be a Marxist–Leninist while pursuing the purges he had learnt from the Nazis. People are very often more disturbed by the idea of change than its component parts. Agreeing to maintain a policy while pursuing your own agenda by stealth can be very effective.
- Do not be afraid to **capitulate**, if the forces of opposition are too strong. In general, though, leaders should not admit that they are wrong even when they have privately changed their minds. Admitting an honourable defeat, however, is much better than seeing your forces devastated.
- Finally, don't overlook the strategy of **biding your time.** It may be the wrong time to risk everything against superior forces, but if you are still convinced that what you are aiming at is right, tactical withdrawal followed by a careful watching brief may be best. The future is likely to bring unpredicted shifts in power and policy, in your opponents' ability and inclination to block your reforms. Wait to strike when they are at their weakest, most accommodating or least prepared.

Failure of market initiatives

What if a particular customer or market initiative has been rewarded only by failure? The first thing is to congratulate yourself and the team on the failure: at least you are trying and you don't want to kill the appetite for another go.

The key thing is to separate out the two main reasons for failure. One reason is that the proposition did not have sufficient appeal to the target market to make it purchase and repurchase the product. 'The proposition' can then be broken down into various elements of the offering, such as price, quality, service etc., to identify the weak link. Remember that you have to overcome inertia and the 'cost to switch' from one product to another, so you will need to have a significantly better offering than that of the incumbent competitors to win business from them. If this first reason applies, you will need to go back to the drawing board, but armed with data from the failure so you stand a better chance of success next time.

The second reason for failure is insufficient effort and/or distribution power to promote the new product effectively. You may find that most of the people who tried the new product liked it and bought it again, but there were simply too few people who fell into this category. This means that you are doing the right thing but just have to put the muscle and money behind promoting the new product. This should be possible, one way or another, even if you have to enter a joint venture with someone who has better distribution, and/or share some of the profits with a bigger brother. Make sure you know whether you fall into this second category and, if you do, do not make the mistake of redesigning your product – an unnecessary waste of resources which will also end in failure.

Killed by a competitor

Sometimes initiatives are blown out of the water at an early stage by a blast from a competitor. A small bank, for example, may offer 'free' banking, or decide to open on Saturdays, only to find that a week later the Numero Uno retail bank does the same thing. Or a company may launch a revolutionary new cosmetic in a pilot area, only to find that the established competitors flood the area with salespeople and special deals in an effort to stop the cosmetic getting distribution.

In a way, competitive reaction, especially imitation, is a tribute to the innovator. It may, however, also terminate the newcomer's business, which is exactly the intention. The aim, therefore, should be to prevent the competitor's reaction in the first place. There are two ways to do this: stealth and cunning.

The stealth approach is to hide your success from competitors, gaining your victories in market share in small or neglected markets which are not much frequented by the competition, which are poorly documented in market research and which are rarely reported on. Even when your presence has been noted, it is often sensible to try to hide the extent of your success, for fear of reaction.

I remember being very puzzled in 1980 to find that although Bain & Company, a fast-growth American management consultancy, occupied five floors of a building in Boston, their name plate was only on floor 3, so a casual visitor would assume that they had only one floor. I commented that this was bad business, as prospective clients might think the firm was much smaller than it was. The firm's founder corrected me, 'Yes, but so too will our competitors. We aim to be bigger than the Boston Consulting Group before they have even noticed that we are coming up on them.'

The alternative tactic, the use of cunning, involves making it very expensive for the competitor to react to you. This may seem a ridiculously ambitious goal for a small or new competitor, but small size cunningly applied has its advantages. As an example, imagine that you can buy certain products much cheaper than the market as a whole, by identifying a particular shipment of a 'once-off' nature that can only satisfy a limited demand. Imagine also that the market is price sensitive. You can then splash out with an introductory offer to customers that is cheaper than your competitors' products and give the impression that you represent real value for money. For your competitor to match your price would be very expensive, because the competitor would have to do it over an enormous volume and for all products.

This strategy of 'matrix pricing' is often adopted by a new competitor, who focuses on the price sensitive segment, well aware that the leading competitor also has a large number of price insensitive customers, but would find it difficult to give some people a low price and not others. Time and time again the leading competitor tries to ignore price competition from a smaller player on the grounds that the latter is an unimportant irritant. This is generally not a wise strategy, but one that firms focusing on short-term profit follow repeatedly, and one that you as a new competitor can benefit from.

If, however, the worst does happen, and a competitor retaliates massively, you should consider all your options before deciding how to respond. Although it may seem cowardly to retreat, this is often the best tactic. Big companies are often slow to respond, but when they do, they can be compared to a herd of elephants, squashing everything in sight. The appropriate response may be to clamber up the nearest tree, keep a low profile, and then regroup with another guerilla initiative.

Bosses unimpressed or hostile

Again, prevention is better than cure.

One golden rule for the new boss is to take tremendous care with upward reporting. This does not mean loading your boss with frequent written reports (which he or she will probably not read) or reporting frequently in person (which can become a nuisance and lead to them 'switching off').

The way to keep your boss on side is devastatingly simple. Work out the few things that are important to him or her (the 'hot buttons') and then feed back results or intelligence that is highly relevant to your boss's own goals. In other words, throw away the usual you-centred view of the world and adopt a boss-centred view for at least part of the time. If you view yourself the way your boss views you, you dramatically raise the odds that you will keep him or her happy.

Do not misunderstand this advice: it is not cynical or intended to undermine your self-respect or have you behaving in a 'brown-nosing' way. The bosses' goals must be legitimate from the company's point of view for you to help advance them. But usually they are legitimate, even though they are usually also not exactly your goals or the way you would think about things naturally. Your boss sees things from a different vantage point. Being responsive to these concerns will help you mobilise support from him or her when you really need it.

But it may happen that you lose your boss's support. Be sensitive to whether this is happening. Very often people try to avoid confrontation and unpleasantness, and are slow to give negative feedback directly. It always comes out, however, and you should watch for the signs. You start to find it difficult to get time to talk to the boss, or he or she avoids eye contact with you, or finds urgent reasons to dash off once you are in contact, or else just behaves in a rather distant, unfriendly fashion.

If this is happening, it is best to take the initiative and ask if you have been doing anything wrong. Have an open and constructive discussion before it is too late.

Unresponsive team

The last general cause of failure is that the team simply won't follow your lead and appears sullen or unresponsive.

If this happens with just one or two individuals, it may be a localised problem. But if you get the feeling that there is a general malaise, the failure is more likely to be yours than theirs. The team collectively is trying – maybe unconstructively – to send you feedback. You should pay attention.

This is not the time (yet) for a cathartic team meeting. Instead, you should talk to one of your team whom you trust most and who will also give a straight answer to a straight question. Ask if you are screwing up and, if so, how.

Remember that if you have a listless and spiritless team now, it is generally not because you have the wrong people – you should have weeded them out long ago. Nor is it natural for people to be passive, unimaginative and lacking in energy: most people, when engaged in what they like doing, are full of life. If the team is not vibrant, you are doing something wrong (they may be too, that is not the point: you are paid to lead and inspire them).

Find out what is wrong and then put it right. It is usually quite straightforward. And failure, as we said at the start, should be a positive part of life, from which you learn. So don't ignore the warning signals or protect yourself from them. Have the confidence, maturity and optimism to confront your failure. You will be happier afterwards.

You are now about to emerge from your two weeks contemplating failure. You should be wiser, stronger and more confident than before. Take the day 80 checklist to see if our course in masochism has really worked.

The day 80 checklist

1 Have you really been able to identify important causes of failure, which you feel are characteristic? If so, list the three most important ones.

2 Have you shared some of your 'failures' with your team and encouraged them to look at their failures in a similar way?

3 Have you identified 'forces of reaction' in your company? Do you have a strategy for dealing with them?

4 What are the two best tactics for preventing competitors' reaction to you at an early stage?

5 How do you prevent your boss withdrawing his or her support?

6 If your team is sullen or unresponsive, is it your fault or theirs, or a mixture of the two?

SCORING YOUR ANSWERS

1 **Yes,** and any three causes is the correct response. Score 20 points.
2 Score 20 points for **yes.**
3 Score 15 points only if you can answer **yes** to both questions.
4 Stealth and cunning (making it expensive for the competitor to respond). Score 10 points for each correct answer.
5 By identifying his or her 'hot buttons' and being responsive to them. Score 10 points.
6 **Your fault.** Score 10 points for this answer and nothing for 'theirs' or 'a mixture' (even though the 'mixture' is one version of the truth, it is far more useful at this stage just to consider it your fault).

INTERPRETING YOUR SCORES

75–100 points Good!

55–70 points Learning from failure is difficult, so do not be too discouraged. Review the points you fell down on.

0–50 points Re-read the whole chapter! Learning from failure is a key skill so do not move on until you have mastered it.

11

Sketching your gameplan

Now is the hour!

We assume that you do not intend to retire on reaching the end of your first 100 days (though a modest celebration may be in order). Now is therefore the right time to sketch out your gameplan for the future.

Many people do this immediately on taking up their bossship. But that is too early, because you can't know the lie of the land at that stage. Think back over all you have learned about the quirks of the organisation and your team over the past 80 days!

Now make use of what you have learned, and reflect also on what is possible and what you would like to achieve. Some bosses never get round to their future gameplan, so they remain at the mercy of events, with only a vague idea of their own objectives. Make sure that you do not join their ranks. However much there is to do and however little time there is to do it in, stop! Lock yourself away and set aside time to reflect on the future.

How long ahead should you plan?

It all depends on the stability or volatility of your economic environment. A month is a long time in a fashion business; a century a short time in the life of a university. But,

unless you have strong reasons for variation, a good rule of thumb is to have a fairly detailed gameplan for the next 12 months, plus a looser, sketchier plan for the 2 years thereafter.

The annual gameplan

This should define what you want to have achieved, with and for yourself, your team and your company, by this time next year. In compiling an annual gameplan you will eventually be putting down crystal-clear objectives, which must be of the type that you can tell in a year's time whether or not they have been achieved. In other words, they must have either quantitative goals or else be of the yes/no variety, where it is clear whether or not something has happened (e.g. 'all members of the team must be able to walk on water by 1/1/95' is a valid objective, because it can be objectively evaluated at your nearest river or reservoir, but 'all members of the team must be interpersonally competent' is not, because it involves a subjective judgement).

Before sitting down to write your goals, though, think about the following questions, which should supply clues about sensible objectives for you.

1 What are you particularly good at doing, so that you can match the objectives to your 'power alley'?
2 Similarly, what is your team as a whole particularly good at?
3 What needs doing, in the sense that it has been neglected or under-emphasised previously, and is important to the running of business and your team's contribution to that?
4 What would get you and the team noticed in your

organisation if you successfully achieved it? What would really make people sit up and pay attention?

5 What could you and the team do that would most help the overall competitive position, strength and smooth running of your organisation?
6 What would you and the team most enjoy trying to achieve?
7 What could be aimed at with a very high degree of confidence that you will be successful?

Pondering these issues should help to generate a list of potential objectives. Then, for each of the objectives on your list, make a column of ticks according to whether the objective satisfies each of the seven questions above. Select the objectives which have the greatest number of ticks, unless you have good reason to do otherwise.

There is no magic about the number of objectives, but seven should be the maximum. There is something to be said for just selecting one very important objective. Most people, however, go for between three and five objectives. Ensure that the objectives have tests or conditions so that, when you come to the end of the year, there will be a black and white answer to the question, 'Did we achieve that objective?'

How are you going to achieve the annual objectives?

It is one thing to have objectives and quite another to know how you are going to attain them. Some guidance may help here:

- Break up the task into intermediate steps, each with its own timetable and targets.

- Ensure that you and the team have enough ammunition for the fight. If it is a matter of obtaining more resource, place your order for this as early as possible, and make sure that it is delivered.
- Communicate what you are attempting to your team (but not beyond it). Make your enthusiasm for achieving the objective infectious.
- Keep the objective in the forefront of your mind every day. Don't let the pressure of events drive it out. Ask yourself (and maybe some of your people) at least every week, are we on track to do this?

All this may sound fine in theory, but a practical example of good annual objectives will probably help.

ANNUAL GAMEPLAN: SWITCHBOARD SUPERVISOR

You are now the new Paris office supervisor of the switchboard of Universal Wisdom Consulting Inc, a swish, high tech American company. There are 52 consultants in the office (a mixture mainly of French, English and American professionals), 16 secretaries and a total of 80 lines. The clients comprise a core group of French subsidiaries of American companies, with a few French and other European clients in addition.

You are a highly ambitious French woman, aged 35. Ultimately you would like to become head of all management services (secretarial and financial) for the office, but you realise the first step in this plan is to provide a stunningly good switchboard service. The service is important, because it is the first point of contact with the firm for potential clients, and because there is a lot of telephone communication needed between the firm's consultants and their clients, and with other Universal Wisdom offices in America and Europe.

Previous heads of the switchboard have lasted a maximum of six months, defeated by the inadequacies of technology and the imperious demands of the consulting staff, who tend to be arrogant, impatient and unforgiving. They live up to their company's name: they are always right.

What have you found out in your first 80 days?

First, you believe that staffing for the switchboard is badly awry. The people used are specialist support staff kept in an unattractive box of an office and rarely let out to wander around or get to know the professional staff. Staff turnover is high and morale low. Of the core staff of three, one was not very competent nor co-operative, and she has been replaced.

Your three staff are now good, but frustrated.

Some of the frustration relates to their isolation, but much relates to the equipment. The telephone exchange is not capable of handling the amount of throughput. In addition, it does unpleasant things, like leaving callers hanging on trying to get through to an extension, and then routeing these unanswered calls back to the switchboard in such a way that the operator cannot differentiate it from a new incoming call. Callers, particularly from other Universal Wisdom offices, often become abusive.

You get on well with the office chief, but he is notoriously mean and vetoes almost all capital expenditure. He guards his cash mountain jealously.

The office is doing well: business is booming and very profitable. One unfortunate side effect of this is that the consultants are often travelling and their secretaries seem unable or unwilling to keep tabs on them, so there is often a long time lag between messages being received at the switchboard and them actually getting passed on to their intended recipients. This, too, generates a lot of nasty feedback.

By day 80 your natural optimism is wearing thin. You obey this book's instructions to think about your annual gameplan, but with a heavy heart. You have now come to the section listing seven issues. The answers you give are as follows:

1 **What are you particularly good at?** Picking challenging jobs, you mutter to yourself. Actually, you are excellent at thinking of the broader business issues and relating them to your job. You could equally well have been an administrator or salesperson as a switchboard queen.

2 **And the team?** Well, the team you have now is good at operating a switchboard, and at giving a personal service to callers and staff. Your colleagues are extrovert and attentive.

3 **What needs doing?** Isn't it obvious, from what has been said above? We need (a) a new switchboard; (b) a new way of working so we can interact with the consultants and their secretaries; and (c) better organisation of the secretaries so that they know where their consultants are at any time.

4 **What would get you noticed?** You are tempted to say, 'If the switchboard worked properly', but then you hesitate. Your experience is that although a bad switchboard gets noticed, a smoothly functioning one does not. The real question is, noticed by whom? You realise that your real client is the head of the office, and you must force him to pay attention to you and the business issues related to your job.

5 **What could you do that would most help the organisation?** Again, the answer you first jump to is 'A

properly functioning switchboard', because you realise how important this is to the firm's image and its ability to do business efficiently. But on second thoughts, the thing that would really help most would be to sort out the entire secretarial system for keeping the professionals' diaries.

6 **What would you and the team most enjoy?** Closer contact with the rest of the firm. And getting out of your hell-hole of the switchboard office.

7 **What could be aimed at confidently?** You greet this question with a wry smile: 'You tell me!' The two key things are to get the equipment and to forge closer links with the rest of the office. If you could crack these nuts, everything else would be straightforward.

THE SWITCHBOARD SUPERVISOR'S ANNUAL OBJECTIVES

Your objectives now stand out fairly clearly. Things will not begin to get better until you have a new switchboard and you need this fast. We will consider how to do this in the face of an implacably Scrooge-like boss in a moment. But there are other objectives too, related to contact with the rest of the office. You write out your objectives swiftly.

1 **New switchboard.** Ensure that a new switchboard meeting the requirements of the office, and able to cope with expansion of the office to 150 lines, is successfully installed and working within the next 3 months (with a specific date).

2 **Contact with rest of office.** Ensure that by (a date 6 months from now) each of the switchboard operators and you know at least 13 of the consultants and 4 of the secretaries (each of your team knowing different people), so that between you, you know all the staff. This objective will be verified by giving the consultants

and secretaries a feedback form, asking whether they feel they know their designated member of the switchboard well enough and whether the service is good.

3 Ensure that (by a date 12 months from now) a new system is put into effect by the switchboard staff to identify where each member of the professional staff is at any time. This will be done either by persuading the office manager to put this into effect or by the individual switchboard staff keeping tabs on 'their' members of staff.

4 Ensure that (by a date 12 months from now) the switchboard staff have migrated from their office to the main reception area, and that the switchboard supervisor is also in charge of reception, so that in the following year a minimum of one reception job can be eliminated at an annual saving of 250 000 French francs.

The reader has probably guessed by now how the mean managing director of the office is to be persuaded to buy a new switchboard. The first plan is to find a switchboard which can be rented or bought at a lower cost than the current one. With the advance of technology and the increase in competition brought about by the recession mentality, this might just be possible. But if it is not, the managing director is to be presented with a plan which cunningly wraps together the extra cost of the new switchboard with a merger of reception and switchboard staff, and the consequent savings therefrom. What self-respecting skinflint could ignore this appeal to the pocket?

The three-year plan

You should by now have compiled your annual gameplan including the objectives and tactics to be used. Now let's consider the extension of this to cover the subsequent two years, so that you have a three-year plan in total.

What should you be driving at for the following two years? This is the time to tackle those issues which you care about personally and which are important for the business, but which it would be unrealistic to try to deal with in the first year.

For instance, in the example above, our friendly but ambitious switchboard supervisor aims to manoeuvre herself into *de facto* control of the reception staff by the end of the first year. She will also, if she and her team achieve their year one objectives, have gained good personal contacts with the professional and secretarial staffs, based partly on the improved performance of the switchboard but largely by building up personal goodwill through being helpful and friendly. Over the next two years, she would like to become overall office manager. This may or may not happen, though, and, in any case, it is not legitimate to put a personal goal largely unrelated to your job in a plan related to that job. But what would be a legitimate goal would be to further consolidate the switchboard/reception staffs to produce new savings, and to prepare a plan for improved liaison/reduction of overlap between the switchboard/reception and the secretarial staff. If the switchboard supervisor can suggest ways in which the effectiveness of the secretarial staff could be increased and its cost reduced, so much the better.

Like the annual gameplan, the rest of the three-year plan should contain objectives (whose attainment or otherwise must be clearly measurable), deadlines and some consideration of tactics to achieve the objectives. There is nothing wrong with having a very short three-year-plan, consisting of the annual gameplan, and a one or two page extension for years two and three. But do be disciplined in revisiting the plan every quarter, noting successes and failures *en route*, and containing any revisions to the plan.

Unlike most other documents of this type, the plan will only be seen by you: certainly not by your bosses and probably not by members of your team. Remember this as you write down your objectives and award yourself marks for their achievement or non-achievement. If you cannot be brutally honest with yourself, the document will be of limited value. But if you can, it should help to keep you focused on what you really want to do, and help to make your working life, and that of those around you, more productive and fun.

The day 90 checklist

1 Have you compiled your annual gameplan and your three-year-plan?

2 Have you thought in detail about how you are going to achieve your annual objectives?

3 Have you ensured that you have enough ammunition for the fight? Specifically, have you requested extra resources already?

4 Have you framed your request for extra resources or other help from your boss in a way that is calculated to appeal to him or her?

5 Do you believe that your team is as keen on achieving the annual objectives as you yourself are?

6 Without looking them up, can you remember your objectives for years two and three?

7 Do you feel confident that you will achieve your objectives for all three years?

SCORING YOUR ANSWERS

1 Score 10 points for each **yes.**
2 Score 10 points for **yes.**
3 Score 20 points if you can answer **yes** to **both** questions; otherwise no points.
4 Score 10 points for **yes.**
5 Score 20 points for **yes.**
6 Score 10 points for **yes.**
7 Score 20 points for **yes;** no points if you hesitate, have a qualified answer or say **no.**

INTERPRETING YOUR SCORES

70–100 points Very good: but the real test is whether you keep the objectives in mind and monitor how well you are doing to realise them.

50–60 points Spend more time to make sure you have a good gameplan.

0–40 points Hmmm. Not good enough. Try again!

12

Reinvest in success

Stay in your power alley

The last two weeks of your first 100 days should be spent in an upbeat mood. This is a time to celebrate what you and the team can do.

Most people try to correct their weaknesses. This is nearly always a losing game: and a depressing one too. There are almost no great leaders in any walk of life who are distinguished all-rounders. All great leaders have great weaknesses and it usually doesn't matter much. The astute manager builds on his or her strengths and rearranges the world around him or her to bring out those strengths.

Reflect on your experience so far

You've now been working as the new boss for at least 90 days. Look back at what has worked well and what has failed. Analyse this in terms of the four categories we looked at earlier:

Experience with . . .	Major failures	Major successes
1 Your team		
2 Other colleagues		
3 Customers/clients		
4 Competitors		

Spend just a little time analysing the failures and what you can learn from these. If the failures reflect your personal weaknesses, you will probably do better to let other members of your team handle these sort of situations than you would to try to reform yourself to handle them better yourself.

But do not brood too long on the failures. Spend much more time now on the right-hand column: the successes! Think what has worked well, particularly where this is the result of team magic – the combination of team members that this has led to things that no individual could have achieved or even believed possible. You should be able to come up with at least three significant examples of team magic over the past few weeks.

Now think along two dimensions. Firstly, think of the common factors in the successful situations and imagine what other circumstances could lead to similar successes. In other words, try to find the playing fields which are your team's natural home. You should then try to imagine ways in which you can find yourselves on such territory.

Secondly, think how you could develop your existing successes further. Could you do more of each success? Could you carry each a logical stage further? How far can you 'milk' each success, while still 'sticking to the knitting'?

To give an example, a team at one of the world's largest merchant banks had developed a particular trading business at which they were fantastically successful. It was very profitable, and although competitors came into this market, the first bank in was able to maintain a competitive advantage, because it had the reputation in the particular niche market and because it had the best traders with the best instincts for which way the market would go.

This successful banking team, however, feared that their market would disappear or severely decline in a few years and started looking round for diversification opportunities. They found a few areas which looked promising, but none which offered the same profit potential as their existing business. Then one morning, one of the traders woke up and thought, 'Are we really making the most out of our existing market?' He talked to his colleagues, and they concluded that the answer was no. Simply by taking larger positions in the markets in which they operated, with very little extra risk, the traders were able to double their profits within two years. As it happened, the market never disappeared or declined either!

This example may seem obvious and banal, but it is absolutely typical. It is appropriate to worry about whether a 'good thing' will last, but it is even more sensible to wonder whether you couldn't do more of what you are doing successfully at the moment.

The power of extrapolation

If you have a clear success to your credit, work out how this can be extrapolated or pursued relentlessly on a wider canvas. If you had your way, how would you expand your scale and scope of operations on these successes? Dream some dreams. Then work out what might just work in practice.

These 'positive reflection sessions' are always much more effective if done with the whole team than with yourself alone. You might want to involve a larger group than just your direct reports, perhaps comprising all of those within your unit if this is logistically feasible.

The power of enjoyment

One of the key secrets of doing anything well is to enjoy it. Most of us have been trained to feel guilty about enjoying things at work: but this training destroys effectiveness quite as much as enjoyment. So seek out things that you and the team will enjoy doing, that can also be turned to the firm's advantage.

What does the team enjoy most? How can you manoeuvre the team into such positions? If you can, and the team is successful, there will be a continuous virtuous circle where the sensation of collective winning leads to greater confidence and teamwork, greater success and so on.

The power of enthusiasm

Life is not a civil service exam. Those who are successful in business are not generally the most intelligent of their class. Those who succeed are generally the most determined, motivated and enthusiastic for their cause. It is easy to be motivated and enthusiastic if you are doing what you like. It is almost impossible otherwise.

Enthusiasm is infectious. It makes obstacles smaller. It brings out extra effort from the team. It conjures up creative solutions where moments before a brick wall loomed. It communicates itself to people in the rest of the firm, to customers and to everyone who can help you in the course of your working day. It creates a current of power which is quite out of proportion to the group's formal authority. It flows and oozes into pockets of resistance, and can corrode the fiercest cynicism. It can, quite simply, change the world.

It follows that the higher the proportion of your day that

you can be genuinely enthusiastic about what you are doing, the more effective you will be. Delegate, reallocate, abdicate or just ignore the rest. But remember that the same consideration applies to the team as a whole, so try to engineer ways in which as many of your people as possible can spend as much time as possible on things that they enjoy and about which they can be enthusiastic.

Make your team a republic of enthusiasm

Your aim should be to have your team clearly more enthusiastic about what they are doing than is true in the organisation as a whole. (If the general level is very low, you should have your team not just exceed the general level, but reach a high absolute level of enthusiasm also.)

You can be sure that you and the team will get noted for your enthusiasm. People elsewhere in the organisation may not have a clue what you and your team does, but the fact that you all enjoy your jobs will attract attention. And, in a quiet way, your team should become a sort of missionary group to the rest of the organisation, seeking by example to convert them to the gospel of teamwork, enjoyment and enthusiasm.

The more that the organisation as a whole absorbs the values of you and your team, the easier it will be for you to lead a larger team and eventually the whole organisation, should you want to do this.

Your 100-day spurs

If you have completed your first 100 days in a spirit of optimism, and if this is shared by your team, this is excellent news and cause for a celebration. Your next 100 days should be easier, because you have already confronted the most serious difficulties with your team, and because the team should be working together more effectively.

It might be in order also to congratulate your team on having survived their first 100 days of you. Having a new boss can be as difficult as being one.

If this book has succeeded, you should already have defused several timebombs, turned around or cleaned out difficult team members, created a real sense of teamwork, improved the service to your customers or clients, strengthened your organisation's overall competence, undermined your competitors, established rapport with your bosses, and focused on doing those things that you and your team are best at and enjoy most.

This is a long list and you may not be sure about all the elements of the Utopia described therein. But the final two-question test is this:

- Have you found new power inside yourself and your team?
- And are you using this new power to help your organisation serve its clientele better?

If the answers are yes and yes, well done! No more tests or words are needed.

Index